BUREAUCRATIC GOVERNMENT

BUREAUCRATIC GOVERNMENT

A STUDY

IN

INDIAN POLITY

BERNARD HOUGHTON

GYAN

Published by

Gyan Publishing House
5, Ansari Road
Daryaganj, New Delhi-110002
Phone: 011-47034999, 9811692060
E-mail: books@gyanbooks.com

Distribution Network
gyanbooks.com
India, USA, Canada, UK, Australia, France

ISBN: 978-81-212-8891-0 (PB)
First Published, 1913

2nd Impression 2023

Printed at: Gyan Press, Delhi.

BUREAUCRATIC GOVERNMENT

AUTHOR: BERNARD HOUGHTON

BUREAUCRATIC GOVERNMENT

A STUDY IN INDIAN POLITY

BY

BERNARD HOUGHTON

Late Indian Civil Service

Quo vadis, domine?

LONDON
P. S. KING & SON
ORCHARD HOUSE, WESTMINSTER
1913

TO

MY WIFE

PREFACE

WHATEVER view we may take of recent events in India and of the forces that inspire them, it is evident we are now confronted with a crisis in her history, a crisis none the less serious because it is long drawn out. The questions at issue relate not merely to details but to the fundamental structure of the Government. The ebb or flow of popular feeling, the sympathy or the reverse with which popular aspirations may be received, may cause fluctuations in the onward movement; but that India's demand for self-government must increase steadily in strength, none who look at the underlying causes can for a moment doubt. The problem before us is how to guide and control that movement, and above all things how to understand it. And to understand it, it is necessary also to understand the system of government against which it is a protest, and which, in fact, is in some sense responsible for its birth. That system is a bureaucracy, perhaps the most perfect of its kind in the world. The present time is therefore opportune for a consideration of the internal working of such a government, and of the advantages and defects which seem inherent in it. In England, too, recent legislation has, for good or ill, largely added to the number of permanent officials, and thereby increased the weight of official opinion in our councils. So the government of a country, where such influences are all-powerful, may be for us also not without interest or instruction.

The plan of the present little work is quite simple. After explaining how in India a bureaucratic government has come to supersede an autocracy, it discusses bureaucracy at first in its more general aspects and afterwards with reference to certain large questions. It seeks for further light on its tendencies in the speeches and acts of a very outspoken Viceroy and in the government of an Indian province. Finally, the present position is examined and suggestions are made for the better satisfaction of native aspirations, while preserving intact the supremacy of England.

B. H.

CONTENTS

FROM AUTOCRAT TO BUREAUCRAT

CHAPTER I

FROM AUTOCRAT TO BUREAUCRAT

When the English step by step advanced across the Indian sub-continent and welded to their empire its teeming plains, they achieved, not a revolution but a conquest. Neither in its origin nor in its framework did the new polity differ in any essential point from those it superseded. It was not as though the conquerors had intruded into a group of ancient states, enjoying free constitutions. Though there were exceptions, the Rajahs and Nawabs, or at least their immediate forbears, had won their possessions at the point of the sword. All, great or small, so far as their spearmen could march or their cavalry ride, demanded from their subjects the obedience of slaves. And, provided the rulers were not grossly tyrannical, their subjects were quite ready to bow without question to their orders, reasonable or unreasonable. That a people should ever have a voice in their own destinies or still less veto any proposed taxation, they would have thought mere midsummer madness. They had been taught from childhood to yield to their kings an obedience far in excess of that dreamt of in our history by the supporters of his sacred Majesty, Charles I. To an Indian, indeed, royalty is more than sacred—it is divine. The English, when they took over the native kingdoms, were careful not to disturb the native reverence for rulers, the growth of so many centuries of submission. It was their aim that this feeling of reverence should be transferred intact to themselves as the new rulers of the land. They therefore sedulously avoided needless innovations, and endeavoured to make their government rather a change of rulers than a change of system.

Doubtless, in the adoption of so conservative a line of policy, the new rulers of India showed much sagacity and practical common sense. When you have entered by force of arms a foreign country and subjugated people wholly alien to your own in race, language, and religious belief, it were folly to accentuate the earthquake shock by gratuitous alterations in the form of government. After the cataclysm of a foreign conquest, the wise ruler may very well be chary of innovations or reform. Nor is it likely that, in taking their stand on the ancient paths and in the continuance in India of an autocratic system of government, our latter-day conquistadores did any great violence to their private wishes and predilections. If, as Mill has it, men ever love power more than liberty, the perils of change to any more democratic polity would appeal to them with convincing force. Be this as it may, in the result the natives of India found themselves under a government distinguished in no vital respect from those under which they had toiled and worshipped, lived and died, through all their weary and forgotten history. Briefly, from the political standpoint, the change was but the replacement of one despotism by another.

Apart from their common ground of autocracy, the English and native Governments resembled each other in their revenue system and other principal features. Of all branches of Indian administration, perhaps the most important is the land revenue, which forms the very sheet-anchor of Indian finance. As might be expected in a vast and heterogeneous population such as that which tills the sun-scorched Indian plains, there flourished under the former regime all sorts and conditions of tenure, with corresponding diversity of revenue systems. From the peasant proprietors of Madras and Bombay and the big landholders or zemindars of Bengal, to the archaic village system of the United Provinces, a variety of tenures, old and new, criss-cross and overlie each other, bewildering as the geological strata which form the scenery of a country. These systems, for the most part, the British Government took on in their entirety. It accepted the existing arrangements as it found them, many years elapsing even before so uncouth a method as payment in kind gave way to cash assessments. An instructive, because modern, instance of this conservatism of outlook occurs in the province of Burma. When in 1852 the Indian Government annexed Lower Burma, they found in existence a capitation or poll-tax, and this they have continued to levy, notwithstanding that such an impost violates all modern principles of finance and presses with severity on the landless labourers. No good reason exists why a poll-tax should be levied in Burma and not in India. Indeed, had not the Burmese kings in the plenitude of their wisdom established it, it is quite certain that the Indian Government would never have dreamed of such a novelty. It must be admitted that at times, by its too earnest avoidance of reform in conquered provinces, the Government of India shows an unfortunate resemblance to the Chinese tailor who, when given an old coat as a pattern, produced with pride an exact replica—rents, patches, and all.

In their administration of India the Mogul emperors, whilst interfering but little with the interior economy of villages—the only self-government the peasants possessed—enforced their orders and decrees through a network of officers, corresponding to the French prefect, who were under the general control of the governor of the province. These officers exercised within their territorial limits supreme executive, judicial, and police functions. It was to them that the governors looked for the enforcement of order, the levy of revenue, and the dispensation of justice. Clothed with these high powers, they represented for good or ill all that there was of government to the naked peasantry; and just as the independence of the governors varied conversely with their distance from Delhi, so did their subordinates wield an ampler authority in proportion to the mileage of ill-kept roads that divided them from the seat of their superior. Under the old regime the discretion conceded to local officers and their freedom from control not infrequently attained dimensions surprising to European eyes. We who have been nurtured in an era of macadamized roads, telegraphs, express trains, and daily posts can only grasp with difficulty the impotence of a Government before the advent of these amenities. Even with their aid in many Native States at the present day the governments present all the features of an advanced case of paralysis. How precarious, then, was such control, how uncertain the execution of orders under the Nawabs and Rajahs who held sway a century ago! You might as well seek for the nervous system of a herring in a jellyfish as expect in these primitive politics modern co-ordination of function.

These, then, were the two cardinal features of the Mogul and of other native systems—the delegation to local prefects of almost plenary powers and the independence of these officers—and it was precisely these features which strike the characteristic note of the early English rule. Really original systems, such as that forged in 1789 by the French *sans-culottes*, gleam in history rarely as white heather on a purple moorland. Human nature, or at least Anglo-Saxon human nature, prefers ever the beaten track, here bridging a ford, or there filling up a quagmire that harasses unduly the honest wayfarer. So with the early dawn of English dominion in India. The sub-governors of the Moguls they transformed into district officers, who, whether under the name of Collectors of Revenue—mark here the emphasis on the financial aspect—or later on of Deputy Commissioners, have since remained the very keystone of the administration.

Though the district officers have since lost, as will be described hereafter, much of their independence and authority, at their inception and for long afterwards they ruled with autocratic power, brooking no interference with their orders. It was the day of plenary authority and of thin-spun control. Woe betide the individual who presumed to belie their supremacy or, greatly daring, presumed to invoke the assistance of powers beyond the district pale! Sooner or later he would rue his temerity. In these, the golden days of the Civil Service, one figures the district officer as riding joyously forth, the virtual lord of his domain, inquiring into grievances, dealing out summary justice, and endeavouring with indifferent success to check the peculation of his subordinates. In a land where much was dark and treacherous he set a bright example of probity, of justice, and of the many virtues of his race. If in his methods he was a little arbitrary, a little arrogant, who shall greatly blame him? The exercise of unchecked power inevitably corrupts some of the finer qualities: it would, we may suppose, in the end tarnish even the pure metal of the Nietzschean superman. And these were just English gentlemen, selected for their culture and intelligence, inspired by a high endeavour to uphold their country's good name in a far off foreign land. The peace that wrapped the land as with a mantle, the confidence in British justice, and the enhanced national prosperity shall be the token and the measure of their success. The fault lay perhaps rather in the system than in themselves that native initiative withered, and native education presented but a stunted growth under the ægis of their sovereignty. For they ruled as kings, and they had the faults of kings.

Before passing on to more modern times it may be worth while to glance at the communications between the Indian capitals and the outlying districts. Properly considered, this matter of roads seems to furnish the key at once to the practical expediency of the old autocratic polity, and to the reasons why this polity has of late years deliquesced and re-crystallized into something which is in essence quite different. To take the case of an average district before the English, as the Hindus put it, manacled India with rails of iron: one not too far away—some outlying districts only received mails once a month—but just a fair average up-country one. Such a district would probably be linked with the capital by a made road, portions at least well metalled, over which postal runners could convey by foot for hundreds of miles the official and other mails. Along this road, from town to town, bullock-carts laden with merchandise, or occasionally with the effects of some official, might slowly crawl, like tortoises on a garden path. Now suppose some ignorant trader aggrieved by what he considered an unjust order on the part of the district officer. If he followed the Oriental method and presented his appeal in person, he would be faced by a weary and hazardous journey, which might extend to weeks, before he could lay his case at the feet of a distant and unknown superior. If he procured a writer to draft a petition for him, he might with reason doubt whether it would ever reach the official for whom it was intended. In either case long months would in all probability elapse before the matter had been reported on and final orders passed. Supposing such orders were not in his favour, he would be thereafter a marked man. This is an aspect of the matter which would appeal to Orientals much more poignantly than the delay, for they have learnt by long and bitter experience with their own officials that a local magnate loves not those who cause his orders to be set at naught. Finally, there was the psychological factor, the reluctance of those days of little travel, when local divisions and influences weighed so much more heavily in the scale than nowadays, to abandon the time-honoured shrines of justice, and to scatter one's incense before strange gods. Small wonder, then, that the peasantry and traders were fain to accept without question the orders of the district official.

Nor were their superiors at the provincial capital likely to interfere overmuch with his discretion. In the case of appeals against his orders, their natural desire to support "the man on the spot" was reinforced by the knowledge that, owing to the difficulties of communication, they could exercise no practical control in his district, and that to sap and undermine his authority would be to destroy what they could in no wise replace. Owing to the same difficulty of communication, inspecting officers, those efficacious means of co-ordinating the different units of government, visited the outlying districts as rarely as angels. The time consumed in travel was so great as to preclude inspecting tours of any frequency. Not, indeed, that, even if practicable, regular inspections by outside officers would have been thought either necessary or desirable. The prevalent conception of government, until quite recent times, was very similar to that of the ancient Romans. Departments were few, and their functions unspecialized. To keep the peace, administer impartial justice, maintain certain roads in good order, and collect the revenues, these summed up not inadequately the whole duty of the district officer. As yet only philosophers and dreamers imagined that a Government might exercise those functions of social service which preoccupy to so marked a degree the thoughts of modern statesmen.

When through this ancient land of India the English engineers laid telegraphs and dug railroads, they little thought that at the same time they were revolutionizing the Government. Yet, given the absence of any consciously countervailing force, nothing was more inevitable than that through this cause the Indian polity should suffer change, and it might with equal certainty have been predicted that the change would be in the direction of centralization of function. In the first place, the telegraphs and the railway postal service enormously facilitated the dispatch of orders to and the receipt of reports from outlying officers. An occurrence in a distant district can now be reported on and orders passed in a few hours by telegraph. Even by post fewer days would be spent in transit than weeks in the olden time. By these means alone the control of the secretariats over distant officers has been so strengthened as to be practically revolutionized.

Then, with increased travel not only are natives less overawed by local authority and local tradition and more prone to appeal, but they have incomparably better facilities for making their appeals. With more numerous appeals the district officer's power of autocratic control has decayed and perished; consciously or unconsciously he has conformed closely to rule. And such rules have not been slow in multiplying beyond all measure. For Governments love uniformity where they are able to enforce it, and secretariats abhor irregularities as vehemently as ever Nature a vacuum. The district officer, far from enjoying the ample discretion and the old freedom of control, running almost into independence, finds himself, like a fly in a web, bound round with regulations and directions on every imaginable subject. He has tended, in fact, towards the same position as a judge on the Bench, whose duty it is simply to interpret an intricate system of law. All possible contingencies, and every conjunction of circumstance, have been foreseen and provided for. It is for the district officer simply to follow the procedure prescribed.

As if further to accentuate these tendencies, inspecting officers increase in numbers, and, availing themselves of the improved facilities for travel, visit frequently outlying districts. Their notes and orders, whilst providing material for new rules, serve as a powerful engine to secure uniformity of procedure throughout the province. One Government will vie with another in meticulous direction of detail. Even the district officers, entering as it were into the spirit of the game, take what their forbears would have considered a perverse pleasure in suggesting new elaborations of procedure, though each new rule shackles still further their liberty. In fact, the real power, the sceptre of authority, lies with the secretariats and the heads of departments, under whose standing or special orders the district officers move and act like marionettes, dancing to strings pulled by an unseen hand. And now the metamorphosis is complete. The Government is a bureaucracy. Impersonal has superseded personal absolutism—the absolutism of a machine, that of the man.

As may well be supposed, the growing centralization of authority did not find in the districts a cheerful acquiescence. Few men give up voluntarily powers which they have long wielded. Many and bitter have been the murmurs of successive generations of officers as they found the bonds of secretariat control steadily tightening round them; and to this day in the intimate conversation of officials no subject gives rise to more caustic comments or evokes more readily the indignant sympathy of the audience. They will never tire of expatiating on the evils of centralization, the lessening personal influence in their charge. Not only do their protests find a sympathetic echo in the public press, which does not hesitate to denounce this development of the administration, but even Government itself with unconscious irony asseverates from time to time the importance of preserving unimpaired the authority of local officers. Nevertheless, the process of impairing such authority has pursued its inevitable course, and it were vain to hope for any reaction or ebb.

Unquestionably, this centralization and co-ordination of work has made for efficiency, for a smoother working of the great government-machine, considered as a machine. Under the semi-absolute rule, which has now passed away, great diversity of practice existed in the different districts. Everything depended on the personality of the district officer. If he were keen, level-headed, and resolute in enforcing his orders, his subordinates would respond to the pressure, and a high standard of administration would be maintained. But, on the other hand, the system undoubtedly had little to check the widespread evils resulting from a weak or lethargic officer. Under such a head, corruption would flourish in the courts of justice like weeds in an untended garden, the revenue would languish, and trade be paralysed by the insecurity of the roads. The intricacies of the present polity have resulted in a higher mechanical level of work, and if an officer is inadequate for the charge, they at least furnish abundant means of ascertaining the nature and extent of his deficiencies. The old personal touch between ruler and ruled is, alas! gone, but, if efficiency be the crown and glory of a Government, then without question the new system is more efficient. The two methods may be not inaptly compared to the small factories, like those near Birmingham, in which the owner works amongst his men, and the large company-owned impersonal concerns which tend to supersede them. The latter possess the biggest and most up-to-date machinery, yield good returns to the shareholders, produce an enormous out-turn, and are aggressively efficient. But . . . ! There is always a "but" in these matters. It will be necessary to probe a little into the soul of bureaucracy —if it have a soul—in order to appreciate the vices that lurk beneath its fair outward show.

BUREAUCRACY

CHAPTER II

BUREAUCRACY

WE have most of us heard of the apostrophe of the Persian King, " See, my son, with how little wisdom a country is governed." We readily applaud its truth with regard to the distressful country mentioned, and still more readily in respect to our own—when the opposite political party happens to be in power.

But, speaking generally, men are prone to ascribe to their rulers, at least in non-popular Governments, a wisdom and prescience far in excess of the realities of the case. In both the autocratic and bureaucratic systems the rulers sit aloof, apart, disdaining to enter into the heat and dust of the controversies that distract the commonalty. Not for them the heated argument, the retort courteous or otherwise, the wrangles and debates of popular assemblies. They repose like gods in splendid isolation. Their subjects know them to be possessed from a hundred official sources of knowledge from which they themselves are debarred. They know them to deal habitually with questions of State, with vast problems involving the destinies and welfare of millions of human beings. Because of their aloofness they, not unnaturally, picture them as supermen viewing from their high places the workaday world with the impartial scrutiny of Olympian gods. Because of their informed knowledge they assume them to be all-wise and all-prescient in their diagnosis of the ills and wants of the common people. And from their constant preoccupation with the high matters of State, they infer in them an expert skill to steer safely the ship of State through troubled waters into the haven of their desire. Excluded themselves from all share in the government, the proletariat looks up with awe and veneration to the exalted beings who control from above its destinies.

Moreover, have not men always loved to fashion idols of their own imagination by way of shelter and protection against the bleak realities of existence, to spare themselves the irksome labour of working out its problems? And bureaucracy is just one of these idols.

For a bureaucracy, like all other forms of government, will be served by human beings not dissimilar from other educated men of their own country. Class prejudices blind them; habits enslave them; inertia clogs their footsteps; they wield no thaumaturgist's wand to waft away human ills. The attitude of detachment they permit themselves, while it envelops them with the glamour attaching to the unknown, must alienate them from the life of the people and blind them to other points of view than their own. The mere fact that they habitually conduct the affairs of government does not necessarily confer on them a right judgment in respect to broad questions of policy. In England lawyers have waged bitter war against legal reform, and the post-office officials obstructed improvements in their department. That officials possess exclusive sources of knowledge may well be conceded. But the cream of the knowledge lies embalmed, if not mummified, in the pages of the bluebooks available to the public—if only the public cares to read them. Reports on special questions are, it is true, often excellent, but, not unseldom, owing to the official bias of subordinates, one sees "as through a glass darkly." In spite of their quasi-judicial tone they lack impartiality.

Consider now the young English official, new-fledged and eager for his work. If he is of the Indian Civil Service, he has probably passed some of the most impressionable years of his life at Oxford or Cambridge, with their oligarchic traditions; if he hails from the Army, still less will he commence his career with any democratic bias. Even should neither of these two general sources of supply have set their hall-mark on him, he will have been educated at one of the fashionable public schools, or, at the least, have spent his early manhood in some haunt of villadom, and in either case have come to regard as an axiom of good government that "the lower orders should be kept in their place." In nine cases out of ten, then, he will start his official career with strong oligarchic leanings. And everything in that career will conspire to accentuate and to reinforce his initial bias. The deference and adulations of the more educated Indians, the cringing obsequiousness of the baser sort, naturally confirm him in the opinion he has formed of his own abilities, and convince him that he really is a Heaven-sent mentor for the guidance of a people walking in Egyptian darkness. In other words, he falls into the snare that Fate ever lays for those who too early in life achieve greatness or have greatness thrust upon them. Being worshipped by others, he ends by worshipping himself. Herod, who made himself a god, was, it is to be feared, but the prototype of a numberless host who in all ages have privately and unofficially deified themselves.

Apart from this influence, which tends to isolate him from the mass of the people, the chief force moulding the young official is the great bureaucratic machine. He finds himself, even at the commencement, placed, so to speak, as a cog-wheel amongst cog-wheels. He has numerous subordinates to whom he issues curt and energetic orders, while he reports more or less voluminously on the various happenings in his charge to his official superior. At first, like an unbroken colt, he may regard somewhat lightly the trammels of his official position; in fact, he is rather apt to take the bit between the teeth. But with the passing of the years, and the insistent stress of routine, he tends more and more to metamorphose into the good official *sans reproche*, though not *sans peur*—for he has the fear of his superiors always before his eyes. He has learnt by degrees that tardiness in the submission of a report or return, or a failure to comply with standing orders as to its contents, calls forth comment every whit as acrimonious as does laxity in the graver matters of the administration, that suggestions tending to the convenience or welfare of the public receive but faint praise, indeed, often an icy welcome. His superiors delight in honouring the bondsman of a faultless routine who understands the rules and gives no trouble. An exact and efficient compliance with orders, whether standing or special to the occasion, is the great desideratum. Originality is frowned on. After a few struggles against destiny and his Deputy Commissioner he acquiesces, and soon wears lightly enough, as silken fetters, the bonds which at first lay on him with leaden weight.

Now, it is decreed that in our complex brains novel thoughts and ideas, forcing their way with difficulty along new nerve-fibres from cell to cell, only emerge with toil and labour, whereas we think with ease along the paths to which we are accustomed. It is this little physiological fact that evolves the trained official. He has become an expert in reports and returns and matters of routine through many years of practice. They are the very woof and warp of his brain. He has no ideas, only reflexes. He views with acrid disfavour untried conceptions. From being constantly preoccupied with the manipulation of the machine he regards its smooth working, the ordered and harmonious regulation of glittering pieces of machinery, as the highest service he can render to the country of his adoption. He determines that his particular cog-wheel at least shall be bright, smooth, silent, and with absolutely no back-lash. Not unnaturally in course of time he comes to envisage the world through the strait embrasure of an office window. When perforce he must report on new proposals he will place in the forefront, not their influence on the life and progress of the people, but their convenience to the official hierarchy and the manner in which they affect its authority. Like the monks of old, or the squire in the typical English village, he cherishes a benevolent interest in the commonalty, and is quite willing, even eager, to take a general interest in their welfare, if only they do not display initiative or assert themselves in opposition to himself or his order. There is much in this proviso. Having come to regard his own judgment as almost Divine, and the hierarchy of which he has the honour to form a part as a sacrosanct institution, he tolerates the laity so long as they labour quietly and peaceably at their vocations and do not presume to intermeddle in high matters of State. That is the heinous offence. And frank criticism of official acts touches a lower depth still, even *lèse majesté*. For no official will endure criticism from his subordinates, and the public, who lie in outer darkness beyond the pale, do not in his estimation rank even with his subordinates. How, then, should he listen with patience when in their cavilling way they insinuate that, in spite of the labours of a high-souled bureaucracy, all is perhaps not for the best in the best of all possible worlds—still less when they suggest reforms that had never even occurred to him or his order, and may clash with his most cherished ideals? It is for the officials to govern the country; they alone have been initiated into the sacred mysteries; they alone understand the secret working of the machine. At the utmost the laity may tender respectful and humble suggestions for their consideration, but no more. As for those who dare to think and act for themselves, their ignorant folly is only equalled by their arrogance. It is as though a handful of schoolboys were to dictate to their masters alterations in the traditional time-table, or to insist on a modified curriculum.

To vary the metaphor, entrusting the government of a country to a bureaucracy is like appointing as captain and mates of a steamship enthusiastic engineers, who have passed all their careers below decks in the engine-room. We can imagine such engineers so wrapt in the intricacies of their craft, the smooth working of crank or piston, as to wholly ignore the steering of the ship, which, for all they know, may be aimlessly circling round and round in the blue sphere of sea. It may even be heading straight for the rocks. The noise of the surf would be plainly audible to their ears were they not absorbed in peering into the engine-room and listening to the well-regulated murmur of the machinery. That is really what the government of a country by a bureaucracy amounts to, the setting of a course and the direction of policy by men who, though admirably versed in the details of government, find it difficult, for that very reason, to take generous and far-sighted views of a nation's destiny. The traditions and prepossessions of a lifetime of official routine must inevitably distort their vision of the more distant horizon. They suffer, in short, from an incurable political myopia.

Owing to their impatience of criticism and passion for docile obedience, a bureaucracy, equally with an autocracy, comes to regard with friendly eyes any institution which inculcates subservience to authority. Habits of obedience fostered in any one department of thought tend to influence by process of analogy the mental outlook on many others. If the human mind is taught to reason or to abstain from reasoning in one large section of its activities, it will act on similar lines with the remainder, consciously or unconsciously. Now, there is one institution that specially preaches reverence for and obedience to authority, and the submissiveness that suffers without complaint. And that institution is religion. It is true that the great organized religions, such as exist in India, inculcate obedience to a Divine authority, transcending the pitiful bounds of our knowledge, and set high above the happenings of the lowly earth. But the principle, the essential element, is the same. Those who are trained to bow down in submission to a heavenly lord or lords—for Hinduism is pantheistic—and to accept with all humility their decrees, are apt to adopt a similar attitude towards the commands of their earthly rulers. Where, as in the great religions of India, religion is interpreted to the laity through priests or a priestly caste, this tendency is accentuated, for here men have become accustomed from childhood to hearing words of authority from their fellow-men and to according them respect and veneration. All three great religions, in fact—Hinduism, Islam, and Buddhism —create a habit of mind eminently favourable to docility towards mundane superiors. And the English rulers of India have not been slow to recognize this fact. It would be untrue—indeed, nothing short of calumny—to assert of them that they have deliberately favoured these religions with a view to paralysing any incipient tendency to criticism on the part of the governed Still less have they had at the back of their minds that last word of the complete cynic: "All religions are equally false to the philosopher, equally true to the man in the street, and equally convenient to the magistrate." Though often blinded by self-interest, the English rulers of India are not cynics. Probably quite unconsciously they have come to recognize that these religions do inculcate obedience, and do as a whole tend to buttress up in the intellectual world the fabric of authority which materially rests on the flashing bayonets of their soldiery. There have, of course, been noteworthy exceptions to this support. In 1857 religious fanaticism, stung to madness by an act of fatuous imbecility on the part of the Army Supply Department, literally shook English rule to its foundations. In our own time Mahratta Hinduism, screening itself behind the name of the freebooter Shivaji, has sought to divert a patriotic and beneficent movement into Anglophobe and sectarian channels. Other and smaller outbreaks, like that of a petty Sikh sect, have been not unknown. Such frothy backwaters cannot, however, affect more than temporarily the steady current of religious fervour which deflects the Indian mind with subtle but insistent force towards an attitude of passive obedience. An attitude of passive obedience is, of course, precisely that desired by an absolute Government, whether autocracy or bureaucracy. In their policy, consistently pursued, of benevolent tolerance towards the native religions, the English have therefore adopted a course which redounded to the quietude of the realm and was in entire conformity with their own guiding principles. It has been one of those happy coincidences when one's duty serves to advance and protect one's own particular interests.

Everywhere the native religions and temples have been protected with a care as scrupulous as it was far-seeing. Apart from the honourable repression of *sati*, the only exception—and an exception which proves the rule—has been the case of the Arya Samaj. Here a religious development essentially puritanical in principle, evinced like Puritanism in political matters, a sturdy independence but little to the taste of a bureaucratic Government. Accordingly, its followers were treated with contumely, the leaders deported or otherwise punished, their proceedings watched with the jealousy of an Abdul Hamid, and all and sundry were given to understand that, although the association remained within the letter of the law, that was the utmost that could be said in its favour. All loyal, all respectable men would do well to shun its contamination. Who can doubt that, had the attitude of the other religions towards authority been different to what it is, they too would have incurred the disfavour of Government?

Closely parallel with the action of the Government against the Arya Samaj is their attitude towards the Indian National Congress. The glittering torch which the one has held up in the domain of religion the other has kindled in the domain of politics. The National Congress has striven to arouse the people from their servile slumber, to incite them to think for themselves politically, to criticize the action or inaction of Government, to remedy abuses, and to originate reform. It is the first-fruits of Western leaven working in Oriental politics. In fact, it has done more: it has created politics in India. To a people accustomed from immemorial ages to timid submission to authority and dull acquiescence with injustice, it has preached the right of private judgment, the right of the citizen to stand forth to criticize the acts of his rulers and to propose remedies. Strange augury in a land of political lotus-eaters! From the rock had sprung forth green foliage, the lifeless desert was filled with the murmur of spring waters. Their discussions breathed a spirit of frank criticism, free from carping or cavilling, a criticism not untouched by a note of sincere and at times well-warranted indignation. It was such a criticism as one constantly hears in England from moderate, not extreme, opponents of the party in power. The reforms they suggested, whether one concurs or not in their present expediency, were the reforms of reasonable and sane observers of Indian politics. Some, such as the reduction of the salt duty and the reversal of the "forward" policy on the Afghan frontier, the Government of India have since adopted with complete success. Others, as the separation of judicial and executive functions, have received their tardy benediction. The speeches and resolutions breathe a spirit of entire loyalty, a touching deference to the British Throne and the British Parliament.

With what welcome has the bureaucracy greeted this first dawn of national life? An enlightened Government would have actively encouraged a political movement so quick with inspiration and with love of ordered progress; a sagacious one would at least have extended to it its countenance. Not so the Indian bureaucracy. For the first time they beheld their monopoly of statecraft openly challenged; for the first time they heard questions of high policy discussed with the frankness and freedom that characterize a parliamentary debate. Sacrilegious hands had been laid on the ark of mysteries. When it became evident that the National Congress had come to stay, the amused contempt which its first meetings evoked gave place to apprehension and some degree of alarm. The epithet "disloyalty," which under a bureaucracy has the same taint as the mediæval "heresy"—an epitome, in fact, of all that is irretrievably damnable—was freely bandied about with reference to its proceedings. It booted nothing that the resolutions passed were studiously loyal, that the form of discussion in no way transgressed the limits of the home Parliament, that more than one distinguished civilian was closely associated with its committees. The mere fact that its members were in opposition, albeit a reasonable and proper opposition, to the Government of India overrode all pleas in its favour. From successive Viceroys, who viewed its proceedings with chilly disapproval, to the jackals of the semi-official press, who have never wearied in traducing and denouncing its proceedings, the National Congress has met from officialdom but "the welcome of war-knives." Bureaucracy has never hesitated to avow frankly its antipathy to everything connected with the Congress. It is undermining the whole structure of British rule; it foments disaffection; better suppress its proceedings summarily than run the risk of an Armageddon in the future. For your bureaucrat, like your thorough-going militarist, suffers from a kind of political dyspepsia; he takes the dyspeptic's gloomy view of future eventualities. If a certain country builds an extra *Dreadnought*, that is a sure presage of a wanton and crushing invasion of our defenceless shores. If in India a native in all good faith denounces some rather obvious defect in our rule, he is clearly the instigator of disaffection, the forerunner of another Indian Mutiny. These worthy people confuse manly independence with disloyalty; they cannot conceive of natives except either as rebels or as timid sheep.

The National Congress, viewed as an instrument for influencing the course of Government, has, it is true, achieved no great success. In this respect it has failed, as before it many forlorn hopes have gloriously failed. John Brown's raid ended in darkness and disaster, yet through it came the war which struck the fetters from the slave. The increased powers of discussion and of initiative now enjoyed by private members in the Legislative Councils will probably divert attention from its proceedings and cause it eventually to die a natural death. But in its educative influence, in its quickening force, in its political inspiration, touching as with a coal of fire the lifeless lips of the Indian masses, converting their quiescence into movement, their torpor into fire, it will live for ever in history as the forerunner of a new dispensation. "The stone which the builders rejected, the same has become the head of the corner."

As was only natural, the relations between Government and the Indian press have not been distinguished by any marked degree of cordiality. A newspaper press is indeed an anomaly in a country despotically governed, whether it be India, or Germany, or Russia. The free traditions and publicity of the press must needs conflict with the secret methods of the despot and his passion for implicit obedience. Hence constant misunderstandings.

In order to appreciate rightly the position in India, it is necessary first to predicate of the Indian press that, like all Gaul, it is divided into three parts. Foremost comes the English newspapers properly so called, edited by Englishmen, reflecting as a rule many of the honourable ideals of the Mother Country, intelligent, practical, and clean. But as a rule they represent merely the non-official Englishman in India, and, where native interests are concerned, they take a frankly partisan view. They criticize the acts of Government with some vehemence when trading interests are jeopardized, but they inveigh far more fiercely against the authorities in cases where, owing to pressure from home or otherwise, they seek to place the native more on an equality with Europeans. They represent, in short, the exclusiveness, the assurance, and the narrow disdain of a privileged class — certainly not India, from the standpoint of the masses.

Next in order is the better class of native newspaper, and the existence of this class constitutes in itself one of the best of omens for the future of India.

Edited for the most part by Indians of good education and imbued with Western ideas, these papers present, with much force, modern and progressive ideas of the art of government. Their general political attitude resembles that of Liberal papers when the Conservatives hold office, only in this case the Conservative Government is perennial and fears no General Election. In the cogency of their criticisms and the breadth of their horizon, they often surpass their English competitors, for the reason that their outlook is national and not merely that of a foreign aristocracy.

Of the horde of petty local papers, chiefly edited by natives or Eurasians, it is not possible to speak in so favourable terms. Depending for their news on papers of the first two classes, they seek to add pungency to an insipid sheet by scurrilities and falsehoods and the inculcation of a settled rancour against the Government. Their inveracities are often amazing. They give credence to rumours and reports the bare statement of which in black and white should suffice for their confutation, in this respect evincing a credulity on a par with that of the ignorant masses. The evil they accomplish is twofold. For not only do they disseminate false reports and false conceptions amongst the lowly masses, but, what is perhaps even worse, they furnish the opponents of progress in high places with an armoury wherewith to combat the efforts of reformers and to justify policies of repression. This backwater in the advancing stream of enlightenment is perhaps not altogether inexplicable. Those who respect others will respect themselves, and there is no surer sign of personal degradation in a writer than the practice of unbridled vilification, the bespattering of others with mud and filth. And when a population has been taught for centuries to cringe before its rulers and to regard itself as the dust in the street in comparison with the majesty of Government, it were idle to expect any high standard of personal dignity amongst its journalists. Only those whom culture has elevated above the mire of their environment can escape its untoward effects. The evil propensities of this species of journalism are therefore likely to continue for some little time. For a healthier tone we must look rather to increased political power and a higher standard of culture, and these are remedies which, though sure, are of slow growth. Yet even in the baser sort of native newspaper it is possible to discover some elements that inspire hope in the future. Even in them one often meets with a true patriotism as distinct from mere hatred of Western foreigners, and amidst much turgid abuse they can formulate at times a perfectly just and legitimate criticism of the actions of officials. In spite of much that is contemptible and nauseating, they yet possess the promise of better things.

The general attitude of a despotism towards the press is sufficiently obvious. It is one of dislike tinctured by diffidence —the diffidence of the polished gentleman towards the small boy of whose actions he is uncertain, and against whom he cannot with dignity retaliate. There is no medicine so distasteful as free criticism to your true despot, whether autocrat or bureaucrat ; indeed, any light of publicity on his proceedings he deprecates as both unnecessary and indecorous. Like the mole, he loves to work in secret, only presenting the finished molehill for the public gaze. But, partly influenced no doubt by their home traditions, officials in India have sensibly enough come to recognize that the newspaper press is a force which has come to stay, and the criticisms of which can in no wise be altogether ignored. Indeed, the existence of the press, whilst it trammels their actions and imposes on them the need of caution, is not without its advantages. For instance, the European press can generally be relied on to support the Government in measures of restraint and coercion against the natives. The unofficial European desires in all sincerity to " keep the natives in their place," and to any measure tending to that goal he gives a ready and whole-hearted applause. The extravagances of the smaller native papers, on the other hand, furnish a ready justification for that majority of officials which dislikes education and views with apprehension the growth amongst the people of broader and more democratic political ideals. One fears that too often, like the crimes of the French Revolution, they have converted those "who should only have been the friends of order into being the enemies of progress as well." It is so easy to quote some empty diatribe or a veiled condonation of crime as an excuse for denial to Indians of the right of citizenship or as a proof of their unfitness to education on modern lines. But, taken as a whole, the press of India remains an entity which the Government would very well do without, if they could. To the end of the chapter the advantages they may derive from it—those it confers on the people are to them relatively unimportant—will appear but as dross when weighed in the balance against the irritation and resentment which its criticisms excite in the official mind. Biologists describe amongst the denizens of the deep a certain catfish whose function in nature is to maintain in health the other fishes by constantly irritating and biting them and keeping them generally on the move. Well, the Indian press is the catfish of the Government of India. And if for that reason only, the latter cannot be expected greatly to love it.

Although officials, and with them the Anglo-Indian press, never weary of asseverating the non-representative character of the native press, unquestionably these papers do portray thoughts and ideas fermenting in the minds of large masses of the population. Orientals do not bare their hearts when in conversation with officials, nor would newspapers flourish with a language and ideology wholly alien to their readers. Alike in the unbridled licence of some and in the obsequiousness of others, we can hear the language of a people for long ages debarred from all that speaks for freedom. There is no greater fanatic than your escaped slave.

For it is not merely through subjection to a series of despots that the virtue has gone out of these congeries of human atoms. Partly through their religious system and partly through the Oriental subjection of women, they have no longer the virtues of free men. As has been already remarked, their religions, which exercise so decisive and dominating an influence over their mental outlook, inculcate in various degrees submission and resignation. The Hindu religion—at least, in its modern form—has through the institution of caste a peculiarly unfortunate effect. What sense of personal dignity and of the nobilities that grace a self-respecting life can be expected from the millions taught to regard themselves as "untouchable," as doomed by the mere fact of their parentage to a lowly and humble servitude? How can we expect even the higher castes beyond the pale of Brahmanhood to talk boldly and frankly with their neighbour in the gate, like the free races of northern Europe? Such institutions, however conventionalized, however hallowed by long custom and tradition, with whatever jewels and sanctities of religion they are encrusted, must cut away the manhood from the nation which really takes them to its heart. But the call of passive obedience in India does not stop with politics and with religion; the family even is instinct with it. Whether in palace or hovel, half of the population spend their lives in learning the meaning of submission to authority, the virtues of docility and humbleness. Women must always, forsooth, bow the head in lowliness, they must fain assume the rôle of those who suffer and who bear. Now, you cannot have a great and really free nation when one half the population are permeated from childhood with the virtues of the slave. You may have a military nation—for man as a fighter is severed from woman by the whole abyss of sex—but you will not, in the true sense of the word, have a great nation. Woman, as has been well remarked, degraded herself, has ended by degrading man. And the school of despotism established in Oriental families colours with its baneful light the whole trend of thought; it emasculates or perverts the self-respect of both sexes.

Small wonder, then, that foreign despots and bureaucrats have found for themselves in India a congenial soil; small wonder that the population has accepted with docility their governance and tendered a ready obedience to their commands. It had been a miracle had it been otherwise, and a sturdy resistance taken the place of submission.

But do not their very moral failings lay a burden of honour upon our bureaucracy? Do they not cry aloud for amelioration, especially from rulers who have always and insistently proclaimed that they exist only for the benefit of the ruled? Surely it might have been thought that they would have hastened to clear away all political barriers to progress and to inculcate, both by precept and by the provision of a suitable education, the seeds of a more generous outlook on life. Alas! the very contrary has been the case. So far from striving to clear the path to a freer atmosphere, they have too often only strengthened the barriers and riveted the gyves that hinder development on more generous lines. The temptation has indeed been great. It is so pleasant to rule over a people entirely amenable to discipline, which accepts without demur rules and regulations however vexatious and oppressive. To guide them to a freer life means so many rebuffs, even contumely and insolence. The bureaucracy has naturally chosen the path of least resistance, which also entirely harmonizes with its own secret inclinations. It is true that it holds out on some distant horizon the vision of a more autonomous nation with freer institutions. But this vision is so nebulous and distant—to borrow the metaphor of a typical bureaucrat, it is like some far-off peak of the Himalayas whilst we are yet traversing the plains—that it really does not enter into practical politics. It is merely a pious aspiration which may or may not hereafter materialize. If the people of India are at school, it is a perpetual school, where greybeards will ever sit at the feet of youthful foreigners, where the syllabus never alters, and where the pupils will pass out at the Greek Kalends.

We make bold to say that by the inculcation of submission, and the crushing of personal initiative, the bureaucracy is inflicting the gravest moral injury with which it is possible for one people to curse another. To deprive a people by conquest of its political independence is an evil, for it wounds its self-respect and enfeebles its vitality; but it is an evil which material prosperity may to some extent counterbalance. But to maintain them after conquest in a state of perpetual tutelage, to treat them as children who shall have no will of their own, whose chief glory shall lie in servile obedience to commands—that is more than a wrong: it is a sin against humanity. It is as though after making a man captive we drugged him with opium in order to keep him quiet and obedient to orders.

For the stultification of national and personal ideals, which results from a despotic system, is nothing short of bedwarfing inspiration in a nation's manhood. Nations advance, a people becomes great not through docility and submissiveness, but by the free play of aspiration and thought, the liberty to advance along all lines of legitimate progress in a self-respecting independence of spirit. That is the very antithesis of the bureaucratic ideal. Efficiency of the machine, not the living organic growth of a people; progress, if such there be, on the initiative of the Government, not progress on the initiative of the people; such are its watchwords.

Since the present King, when Prince of Wales, shrewdly remarked that more sympathy was required between the ruler and the ruled, another spirit has tinged, it is true, official utterances; but one fears that there has been little more than lip sympathy. To quote the words of Mahommed Haque in the Viceregal Council relative to non-official proposals: "We get an enormous amount of sympathy from the official side, and afterwards they [the proposals] are all unceremoniously thrown out." One should not, indeed, expect condolence from a piston-rod nor look for the exercise of loving-kindness in a locomotive. And therein lies the flaw in its armour whereby a bureaucracy fails to inspire the sense of loyalty which is so often the birthright of an autocrat. Men, even the most virile and independent, love to have as their chieftain a human being like themselves, greater, wiser, more prescient if you will, but still a human being subject to the same passions, tarnished even with some of the same weaknesses as themselves. It is this emotion which supplies the well-spring of loyalty to kings, and which draws men in their reason's despite to follow the fortunes of political adventurers. The coldly correct formalism of a bureaucracy chills all feeling of devotion to the Government just as the bitter wind of spring the opening flower-bud. Men obey it as they obey the time-table of a railway, but without enthusiasm, and with a dreary sense of impotent dislike. Here, then, lies the third defect of the Government of India. In addition to the necessary bane of a foreign domination and the gratuitous evils springing from its system of repression and tutelage, it is destitute of the human touch that can link the sympathies of the ruled to their rulers, and that atones for so many shortcomings. Can we wonder at the more emancipated spirits beating themselves against the granite walls of their prison with bitterness and despair, aye, sometimes with crime and dark iniquity?

BUREAUCRACY

CHAPTER III

BUREAUCRACY (*continued*)

OF all departments of its activities perhaps education furnishes the true touchstone by which we may best judge the claims of a modern Government to be considered progressive and enlightened. The days when rulers held the education of the people to be no concern of theirs are fast fading into oblivion, as the mists of night vanish in the light of the new day. All Governments, or at least all civilized Governments, profess a solicitude for education, even when they most notoriously neglect it. What is the record of the Government of India in this matter? Under what stars have they steered their course, and how far have they discharged the burden which lay upon them to educate the millions under their care?

To understand the policy followed by them in this matter, it is necessary to understand the ideas regarding popular education which sway the class from which the Government is recruited. Though now falling into discredit, a very important and widely spread theory is based on a certain view of heredity. In the sphere of the mind it attaches great weight to somatic inheritance, which is held to determine the scope of individual acquirements. Because the proletariat of a country has been sunk for centuries in ignorance and superstition, has never even knocked at the door of knowledge, it is supposed that it is unadapted by constitution to receive instruction. In this view to open wide the door to the ignorant multitudes would be to give them food to which they were wholly unsuited. It may lead to disloyalty, to social unrest, even to general chaos. In accordance with their inherited aptitudes, the commonalty are conceived of as enjoying in peace and thankfulness the fruits of their labours, contented with their lot in life, and neither aspiring to nor desiring that education which a well-ordered social system bestows so lavishly and with such beneficial results on their betters. 'Tis a pretty picture, as true to reality as the Watteau shepherds and shepherdesses. Unfortunately, if you have ignorance you will also have stupidity and crime and cruelty. In so far as you deny to men knowledge you give scope in them for the ape; you rob them of all those graces and amenities which in your own case constitute the pleasures of existence, all that makes life worth living. These and many other evils inevitably flow from a refusal to educate. Those idealized pictures of Arcadian life are for the most part only the dreams of self-satisfied dreamers. In actual fact you will have wholly unnecessary suffering and misery, physical as well as mental. Nevertheless, modern arguments for popular education now, only with difficulty, gain ground. The old false ideas, such as we find in Aristotle's distinction of "free" and "slave" natures—as though it was not their environment which makes men dare as free men or cringe as slaves—are still secretly cherished by many who claim to be educated and intelligent. These ideas have influenced beyond doubt many officials in their attitude towards education in India. They sympathize with the natives in their unfortunate lot; but they do not pause to reflect what would have been their own character or outlook in life had they themselves been brought up in a Tamil hamlet, or conversely, how different would be the mental attitude of a Sudra had he been educated in an English public school—and to draw the obvious corollary.

Apart from these false views of heredity, officials in India are liable to a special bias on the subject of education owing to the sources from which they are drawn. It must be admitted that neither Oxford nor Cambridge nor the Army have been distinguished for any great zeal in the cause of really popular education. They stand for aristocratic and exclusive ideals, not for the democratic hope of an equally educated nation. Their pupils are profoundly impressed with the danger of a little knowledge; in fact, they seem to regard education as though it were some potent medicine, to be administered only by the most skilful physicians, and even then with caution and misgivings.

Clearly, then, officials in India have received no antecedent bias towards a general diffusion of education. And what little fervour may still remain in them, official routine and bureaucratic influences will probably chill to freezing point. To a bureaucrat, education, unless confined within the strictest limits, is of necessity odious. If you educate the proletariat, if you scatter schools broadcast, you prepare the ground for the dissemination of all kinds of disloyalty and upstart ideas, you make people critical and impatient of official control, and, worst of all, you teach them to be independent and to think for themselves, quite possibly on lines which officials regard as pernicious. All this is wrong, very wrong. Much better that they should retain their traditional docility to rulers, who alone know what is best for their subjects. Once the people really begin to think for themselves, it is impossible to say to what lengths they may be led, what crude and ill-advised ideas may begin to ferment. The office of Government, or at least of a bureaucratic Government, is to guide and control the people, and an educated people is notoriously impatient of control from without. Indeed, a certain school of officials openly ascribes the present unrest in India to education, which it deplores as the prolific seed-bed of sedition and disloyalty. An inspector of schools in an official brochure, whilst praising the work done by his department in the Central Provinces, has been careful to explain that it did not attempt to make the pupils anything save that for which Fate intended them. "For which Fate intended them!" That is a truly official impression of education. Not to raise them up, not to kindle ambitions, not to inspire virility and independent thought, but to keep them humble and docile in strict subordination to Government.

The debates on Mr. Gokhale's Bill for the extension of elementary education provide us with an example of this official attitude. This Bill for making primary education compulsory in selected areas, was so cautiously framed, and contained so many safeguards, that in all probability, had the Imperial Government accepted it, it would have remained a dead letter in more than one province. No one who has studied its provisions but must be impressed by the extreme, almost timorous, desire to avoid precipitancy, and to yield in every way to local susceptibilities. The following table gives the opinion of the individuals and bodies consulted :—

	For.	Against.
Non-officials ...	95 per cent.	5 per cent.
Indian officials ...	39	26
English officials ...	51	118
Local Governments	none	all

It would be impossible to illustrate more clearly the cleavage between official and popular opinion. Alone of the various classes, the local Governments, which in practice represent the secretariats—the quintessence of bureaucracy—are unanimous in their opposition; the English officials are less so, but still with an overwhelming majority; the Indian officials, though probably influenced by their superiors, are in favour of the Bill; whilst non-officials almost entirely acclaim its provisions. The local Governments had, it may be recalled, previously negatived a proposal for free primary education, although it enjoyed the support of Lord Minto. As for the reasons given by them, they recall nothing so much as Lord Morley's sketch of the man of the world, with "his cordiality towards progress and improvement in a general way, and his coldness and antipathy towards each progressive proposal in particular." The Burma Government, indeed, distinguished itself by the grotesque assertion that "there was already a sufficiently large advance of education in the province!"

The official attitude towards a Bill so moderate and so cautious as that of Mr. Gokhale fully explains the halting progress made until quite recently in Indian education. In the quarter of a century from 1882 to 1907 the percentage of pupils to the population only rose from 1·2 to 1·9 per cent. Though the expenditure on civil departments had increased to 10 crores, and on the military department to 32 crores, education in 1907 received a bare 93 lacs—*i.e.*, less than one crore. In view of these facts and of the admitted ignorance, superstition, and credulity of the Indian masses, how sadly ironical must appear the declaration of the Court of Directors in 1854 that the education of the people was one of their most sacred duties, how empty the assertion by successive Viceroys of the necessity for an increase in the provision of schools! Mr. Gokhale, indeed, made one mistake in the arguments in support of his Bill. He urged that however limited its scope, it would at least educate the people to the advantage of public instruction. It is not, however, the people who require education in this matter: it is the officials, and in particular the secretariats.

Had the finances of the country been

gravely embarrassed during the past thirty years, or had it been engaged in a death-struggle with foreign invaders, there might have been some excuse for the slow progress made. The officials in India might with justice have demurred to following too hastily the example set by the mother country, and even by Japan. But this was not the case. It is true that prior to 1899 the military party at Simla inveigled the Government into many expensive and futile frontier wars, and that up to the same year the falling value of exchange entailed a heavy charge on the revenues. Very much more might, however, have been effected in respect to education had the Government been really zealous in the matter. Notoriously it was nothing of the kind. From 1899 onwards, owing partly to the wise frontier policy instituted by Lord Curzon and partly to the fixation of exchange, the Government has been in a position of relative affluence, and it is just here that the sinister interests of a bureaucracy have been so strikingly in evidence. Instead of hastening to remove the stigma of obscurantism cast upon the British rulers by the ignorance of their subjects, they showed, by the increase of salaries and the multiplication of posts, that it was the working of the machine rather than the advance of the people that lay nearest to their hearts. Expenditure in every department went up by leaps and bounds. One and all crowded to dip their hands into the lucky bag. "I do not believe," Sir E. Baker remarked in 1907, after five years' service as Finance Minister, "that one single day has passed in which I have not been called upon officially to assent to an increase of pay of some appointment or group of appointments, to the reorganization of some department or to an augmentation of their numbers. . . . Nor are the members of the various services at all backward in urging their own claims." There is a story that in one province an Inspector-General, when asked by the Police Commission whether he had any alterations to suggest, declared that the only alteration necessary was an increase in his own salary—which he got!

However, this rain of rupees, which fell so plenteously on the just and unjust amongst officials, stopped short of the public schools. Money is naturally spent on what interests one most, and education, to say the least, does not interest the average official. One country gentleman with a taste that way may spend the bulk of his income on a large staff of retainers, and may scrimp the other items of his expenditure; another may favour a great house and a perfect garden; another entertainments; whilst a fourth may devote his income to the education of his children. No revenue in the world will suffice for all the possible activities of an administration. Each Government lavishes money on those objects which appeal to it most. The plea of want of funds, so frequently put forward, simply means that, in the opinion of the Government, there are other and more eligible objects on the furtherance of which it prefers to devote its revenues. Hence in India education has ever been a Cinderella in rags and tatters owing to "want of funds."

Fortunately, another page has of late been turned in the chapter of Indian education, hitherto so discreditable to the fair fame of British rule. Thanks to a Viceroy who has the statesmanship to place education with sanitation in the forefront of his programme, and to a really zealous Minister of Education, a new era has now dawned. A bold and generous extension of Primary Schools, together with the establishment of many needed universities, are the cardinal features of the policy to which the Government of India has definitely committed itself. Educationists may now look forward to the future with more of confidence and hope. The measures taken constitute, it is true, but the plinth of a yet inchoate edifice, but they are a noble plinth; they form the substratum of a system of education at once worthy of the British Government and adequate to the needs of the people. The essential matter is the change of policy. And for this the credit must be ascribed to Mr. Gokhale and the devoted band who have laboured with him, in good report and evil report, to urge upon an indifferent Government how the people perish for lack of light. They have for the time served their country "more by their failures than by their successes," but the time cannot be far distant when the policy of free and compulsory education, emblazoned on their banner, shall become an accomplished fact. When that victory comes, India will not forget those who have so long borne the burden and heat of the day.

We have seen that when the fixity of the rate of exchange and a statesmanlike frontier policy set free large sums of the public revenue, the great proportion of the surplus thus made available was lavishcd, not on education but on the emoluments and resources of other departments. One of the chiefest of these was the Army. It might have been thought that with the end of the frontier wars and the crushing defeat of the Russians in Manchuria, the grievous drain into this abyss would have ceased. But your true militarist is essentially a man of resource;

he is ever ready with some facile device to startle the timid with the gorgon face of war. And a bureaucracy is always especially sensitive to such a menace, whether it comes from within its boundaries or from a foreign foe. With an uneasy sense that in spite of the many benefactions their rule brings to the people, they have not these ingrates at their back, they readily take alarm at the thought of war and strive to make themselves doubly and trebly secure against all possible eventualities. It is significant that until quite recently, whilst education had no special representative in the Viceregal Council of Seven, the Army alone of Government departments had two. The Commander-in-Chief has also occupied in India a vastly more important position than, for instance, the Secretary for War in our own Cabinet. When on one occasion he insisted that Russia was never more dangerous to India than after she had received a sound thrashing at the hands of Japan, this incredibly absurd proposition was accepted by the officials without demur, and the stream of money so sorely needed for education and internal development continued to pour, at an accelerated pace, into the bottomless abyss of the frontier and of military requirements generally. That the Japanese war nearly resulted in a revolution in Russia, that the structure of her bureaucracy shook to its foundation with the strain put upon it, that her finances were in such disorder that no Czar out of a lunatic asylum could dream of another war for many long summers—all this counted for nothing. Just as at present, when the German scarecrow is still flaunted in our eyes, although the Balkan war has transformed European politics and placed Germany on the defensive between a Chauvinist France and the giant army of Russia, so did the Government of India continue with an insane energy its expenditure on the North-West Frontier after all chance of an invasion was passed. Russia is now our very good friend—though the peoples of Persia and China may well wish otherwise—and the Russian scare has disappeared from India, until the next stampede. But the increase of the military expenditure by rapid steps to thirty-two crores, about two-fifths of the total revenue, is the measure of injury this scare has inflicted on India. This at a time, be it noted, when Government spent less than one crore on education. India, it must be remembered, is no Crœsus like England, but a very poor country. The average annual income is less than £2 per head as compared with £20 in England. Even with the assistance of the land revenue, the resources of taxation are severely limited, and many most urgent wants must needs remain unsatisfied. To devote two-fifths of the total revenue to the Army meant the starving of education and the loss of millions of lives through quite preventable disease. It is no exaggeration to say that Russia has caused infinitely greater evil to India by the menace of war than she can ever achieve by war itself.

Of the various "reorganizations"—euphemism for increase in numbers and emoluments—that have recently sucked up like sponges the surplus revenues, the secretariats have, as might be expected, taken their ample share. A bureaucracy always tends to an undue development of this branch of administration. As the virility, whether official or popular, of the country at large decays, the secretariats wax and grow mighty. This is only natural, for these departments are the very core of the bureaucratic machine. When the efficiency of that machine becomes the highest aim, for them at least money will never be stinted. The number of covenanted civilians in the Government of India has increased from fifty-five in 1892 to eighty-five in 1910, and the total secretariat charges of that administration alone aggregate thirty-three lacs per annum. Further, the Simla officials bid successful defiance both to the Public Service Commission and to the reductions made under Lord Hardinge's orders. The evil does not stop with the mere wastage of public moneys. An overgrown department naturally multiplies its own activities, overlooks everything with a grandmotherly care, and seeks to draw into its own hands the controlling strings in the pettiest matters. Thus we have Lord Minto complaining that he was expected to overrule a local Government in respect to the purchase of a horse valued at Rs. 70, and to check the expenditure due to the erection of a bathroom. Well might he have echoed the despairing cry of the Czar Nicholas, that Russia was ruled by ten thousand clerks! For the secretariats are the very apotheosis of clerkdom, and they tend to infuse in those who labour in them a clerk's mean outlook on public policy. For this reason the fact, naïvely admitted by Lord Curzon, that Lieutenant-Governors and other high officials are usually drawn from among the secretaries, and spend their early career in "devilling" in secretariats, has a certain sinister significance. Men so trained and brought up in such surroundings naturally tend to perpetuate the evils of a bureaucracy. So far from taking broad and generous views of the aspirations of the people, they are more likely to place in the forefront official views and official interests, and to regard official convenience as outweighing the public good. The whole matter moves in a vicious circle, which nothing but strong outside pressure can break.

Akin to the overgrowth of the secretariats is the custom of their annual migration to the hills. In these halcyon abodes, remote from the heat and dust of everyday life, the high officials and their offices spend quite half the year. The proportion varies from nearly two-thirds with the Government of India to a little over one-third with the Central Provinces' Government. No subject is more hackneyed or forms the subject of more trite comment in the Indian press. Yet the matter really is one of very grave importance. In the first place, there is the alienation of Government from the common people. The position has been well described as though after the Japanese had conquered England, the Government established by them were to spend the greater part of the year in the

Riviera. Would not such a procedure alienate the sympathies and embitter the disloyalty of the great mass of the people? How can we expect loyalty and affection towards rulers who so ostentatiously withdraw themselves from the life of the ruled, as though they disdain common cares and common troubles? Of course, the migrations to the hills are supported by such arguments as that the efficiency of the heads of departments and their officers is of vital importance to the welfare of the country, that their brains work more clearly in the cool air, like the Grand Lunary in H. P. Wells's fantasie, and that therefore it is to the public advantage that they should spend the hottest months of the year in these retreats. No doubt the officials honestly believe in the validity of such contentions. *On croit facilement ce que l'on aime ou ce qu'on désire.* But the argument will not bear close inspection. The Burma Government, for instance, has only recently migrated to the hills, yet no one will assert that the output of the secretariat before this innovation was one whit inferior to that of more recent years. It is admitted that most Europeans in the plains, with the aid of liberal leave rules, manage to discharge efficiently their duties, and to maintain a reasonable standard of health. Much more, then, should this be the case in the presidency towns, with their many modern amenities, and with the palatial offices the Governments take care to provide for themselves. Indeed, there is a certain element of dishonesty in these migrations. The high pay of Indian officials is intended in part to compensate for the discomforts of a climate which, though not unhealthy —apart from zymotic disease—falls, as regards comfort and amenities, far behind that of England. Yet these high salaries are continued after such officials have, by the device of hill migration, contrived to enjoy a climate not inferior but much superior to that of the mother country. No men in the world are impartial judges where their own interests are concerned.

In the second place, the segregation of the Governments during half the year in these remote retreats exerts a subtle but baneful influence on the character of the officials themselves, and through them on the Government. It deepens and intensifies their officialism. To understand this we must take an example from another sphere. In those countries which hold by the priestly ideal in the exercise of their religion, the people sharply distinguish between the parish priests and the members of the great monastic orders or brotherhoods. Whilst the parish priests enjoy a rich dower of veneration, of love and respect, a settled hostility is often the portion of the monks. Why is this? Priest and monk both follow the same dogmas, they worship at the same shrine, they are members of the same Church. The reason seems to lie in the fact that whereas the parish priest lives amongst the people, and is, so to speak, one of themselves, the monks live aloof, segregated from the commonalty, and in close contact with the other members of the same order. Hence they come to place the interests and aspirations of their order first, and those of the laity a remote second. In quite recent times the Philippinos gave a striking example of this difference of attitude during their rebellion against the Spanish. They spared the priests but wreaked horrible atrocities on the monks, whom they accused of caring for nothing but the aggrandisement of their orders. We have seen a similar attitude in France and in Portugal; both of these countries have expelled the orders, whilst leaving almost unmolested the parish priests. And other examples of strong popular feeling on the subject occur in history past and present, notably in Spain, Germany, and our own country.

Now, in its mental outlook a bureaucracy has much in common with a sacerdotal system. There is the same aloofness from and sense of superiority to the common people, the same belief in their own omniscience, the same kindly benevolence to the laity if only they accept unquestioned the guidance of the elect. On the other hand, criticism inspires in each case an angry impatience, the people or laity being conceived of as ignorant, and shut off by an impassable barrier from the practice of the mysteries. It is not without cause that the Indian press stigmatizes the Simla officials as an hierarchy. A bureaucratic polity is a sacerdotal polity. And the segregation during a large, sometimes the greater, part of the year of the various Governments in sequestered hilltops is closely analogous to the segregation of monks on sacred mountains.

In those cool and remote hills, where the hum of the outside world serves but to add piquancy to the solitude, officials must needs look on themselves more than ever as beings apart. The tranquil official atmosphere envelops them as with a cloud, unruffled by the rude breath of public criticism. In its luminous haze all official acts appear transfigured, official opinion seems the sublimation of wisdom, official interests strike as of dominant importance. In wisdom and foresight they come to think themselves and their coadjutators as much elevated above the rest of humanity as are the mountains above the sea-level. They develop a kind of official "herd suggestion," which results in an attitude quite divorced from that of the public—shall we say laity?—and even of the district officials toiling in the heat below. Whatever faults of self-sufficiency the Government formerly possessed will have multiplied most certainly ten-fold. It would, indeed, be hard to devise any measure more calculated to aggravate the mischief of a bureaucratic Government and to perpetuate its vices than this system of migration to the hills.

Although the propinquity of Delhi to Simla and its excellent climate, figure in Lord Hardinge's despatch as two minor reasons for the transfer of the winter capital of the Government of India from Calcutta, no one who knows the official mind will doubt the weight of these considerations in the counsels of his advisers. True, Delhi was the former capital of the Mohammedan conquerors, and famous Hindu kings had reigned in its vicinity. But this argument invites the obvious retort that both Aryans and Mohammedans, invading India as they did from the north-west, naturally fixed their capital where they were strongest. The English, on the contrary, came from the sea, and the sea is our natural strategic base. Moreover, since those times the whole social structure has changed. The centres of trade, of civilization, and of enlightenment lie, not in the remote interior but in the great seaports. It is just this fact which constitutes the decisive argument against the Delhi site. Spending as it does the greater portion of the year at Simla, the Government of India did live some time, if only a meagre five months, at Calcutta, where it came into bracing contact with non-official opinion both native and European. Such contact, however distasteful to the official mind, is in reality the most wholesome of medicines. All this will now be changed. The purely official environment at Simla will merely alternate with one a little less so at Delhi. The Government of India must move more and more in an orbit remote from the life and interests of the people it governs; it must be yet more saturated by official traditions and influenced by official interests. Since both its summer and winter capitals will lie in the Punjab, it will in practice—though not, perhaps, in theory—be mainly recruited by civilians from that province. Now, the Punjab is educationally the most backward province in India, and its officials are influenced in a special degree by militarist as opposed to popular traditions. This argues ill for the supremacy of progressive ideas in the counsels of Government.

Before passing on to other matters, a comparatively minor point, which, however, may fulfil the purpose of the proverbial straw, seems worthy of notice in connection with the provision of bungalows for use on official tours. In most provinces these have increased beyond measure in recent years. In India tents, and in Burma zayats, met the modest requirements of the old-time officer, but these apparently no longer suffice; roomy and well-furnished bungalows are everywhere demanded. With a Pactolus' purse there would be, of course, no serious objection to their construction, but, as is well known, the very contrary is the case. Constructed as they are for the most part from the District Cess Funds, every rupee spent on them is one taken from the crying needs of education and of sanitation. Even their legality is in many cases questionable, since, although the Cess Fund rules permit buildings for "travellers," in many places where these bungalows exist the only travellers are a few casual officials. It is merely another instance of the unfortunate bias of the latter where their own interests are involved. The Tanjore District Council in Madras, more independent than most, has, it is instructive to note, recently refused point-blank to continue the maintenance of these buildings.

That a right judgment in matters of detail necessarily infers a right judgment in questions of policy, a premise tacitly assumed by some defenders of bureaucracy, seems a sufficiently obvious fallacy. It is easy to cite examples in India where despised native opinion has been right and the officials wrong. The question of education is one. But education is not the only great question of policy in which officialdom, so far from speaking words of wisdom, has erred. Take the case of the Salt Tax. Again and again sessions of the National Congress have inveighed against the heavy incidence of this tax on the starving masses, and have urged its reduction. Mr. Gokhale and others advocated the same course in Council. In support of its usual attitude of *non possumus*, officialdom argued that in practice the annual tax paid by even the poorest, was so trivial that it could make no difference in their consumption of this necessity of life. In 1903 and again in 1905 Lord Curzon's Government, pressed by public opinion, did make reductions in the taxation of salt. What was the result? In each case the reduction of the tax was followed by a substantial increase in the consumption of salt *per capita*, thus demonstrating the truth of the non-official contention and proving that the tax had really restricted the use of salt amongst the poor.

Another plank of the National Congress, and a favourite theme of many Indian publicists, has been the separation of judicial and executive functions. The union of these jarring duties in the same person, they argued, unconsciously biased his attitude as magistrate or judge, and impaired the confidence of the people in the impartiality of the judicial system. The system is, it will be recollected, a survival from the former native and early English regime, where an officer combined in his own person many diverse functions. Survivals die hard. Obviously a system of this kind lends itself to abuses. When an officer is responsible in his executive capacity for the preservation of order in the whole or portion of a district, he is likely to punish with peculiar severity offences affecting that order or involving recalcitrance to officials; in cases where the evidence is nicely balanced, he may, from an unconscious bias, decide in favour of that for the prosecution. Even a Chief Judge (a civilian) has been known in Rangoon to give as a reason for his opinion on an important legal point that a contrary decision would cause inconvenience to Government. The validity of these objections has, however, been always vehemently denied by officials, who see in this separation of functions a loss of prestige and a diminution of their own authority. Nevertheless, the Government of India—largely, one suspects, on the initiative of Lord Minto or the Secretary of State—has recently admitted that the separation of judicial and executive functions is advisable. Partly for financial reasons little has yet resulted from this pronouncement, but the admission of the principle, so long and contemptuously denied, will always stand as a landmark in the history of India.

On the question of the Councils, too, official opinion has proved to be wrong. The credit, or at least a part of the credit, for the recent generous enlargement of the Indian Council was indeed ascribed by Lord Minto with characteristic modesty to the bureaucracy. But beyond doubt officials throughout the country scowled at the measure actually formulated; at most they advocated the creation of an advisory Council, carefully selected from the more conservative elements, and shorn of any real power to check the working of the machine. For this successful and statesmanlike measure the thanks of the public are in reality due to himself and Lord Morley, especially the latter. Amongst non-officials, Mr. Gokhale contributed in no small degree to moulding it in the form it was ultimately cast. Bureaucracy, so far from assisting in the birth of this reform, has done its best, by narrow and illiberal regulations, to curtail its scope. Nevertheless, when one recalls the vehement outburst of race hatred that disgraced officialdom, in common with the European population generally, during the debates on the Ilbert Bill in 1883, there is much cause for congratulation. The dragon of racial arrogance, if still alive, has sheathed its claws, its splutterings have lost much of their venom. Though officials still view with dislike the growing power of natives, they at least take care to express their opinions with moderation and tact. All this is much to the good. Perhaps, to use an expression of Bagehot's, it indicates a change in the "climate of opinion"; perhaps it may be the first forerunner of a just equality of treatment unthinkable to the old type of Anglo-Indian.

If a bureaucracy, with absolute honesty and integrity of purpose, sometimes gives priority to its own interests and its own requirements before those of the commonwealth, it can deal faithfully enough with other sinister interests. And surely in an imperfect world this should be accounted to it for merit. Even representative or partially representative Governments, such as that of England, frequently allow themselves to be influenced by forces hostile to the general welfare which would receive but short shrift in India. In the Post Office the cash-on-delivery system, the only reform advocated by Mr. Henniker Heaton, baffled by extra-official influence, has long been established in India. Here the opposition in England sprang from the petty shopkeeper, whose outcry overrode the manifest advantage to the population generally. Again, two legal reforms, the codification of the law and land registration, have made but slow advance in England, thanks to the opposition of the legal profession. India, on the other hand, stands in the front rank of nations in both respects. The most malign and powerful of all, the vested interests in the sale monopoly of alcohol, have never been permitted to spring up in India. Licences are sold for one year only, and it is clearly understood that the purchaser has no vested interest beyond the year for which he buys. It is true that in many instances both the Government of India and the provincial Governments—notably that of Bengal—have conducted their excise policy with an eye, not so much to temperance and sobriety as to the augmentation of their own revenues.

It required a resolution of the House of Commons to destroy the pernicious outstill system. In spite of protests to the contrary, considerations of revenue yet cast a Brennus sword into the scales when questions of excise policy are weighed. Both in the excise and in the opium administration there is much hypocrisy, little of noble and national ideals. Still, the absence of vested interests is an asset of enormous value. The Government of India possesses a perfectly free hand in this great department, and, dowered with this advantage, it may attain even yet, though perhaps in a remote future, results comparable with those achieved in China and in Japan.

A BUREAUCRATIC VICEROY

CHAPTER IV

A BUREAUCRATIC VICEROY

If some thirtieth-century Mommsen should seek a pattern from which to model the soul of a bureaucrat and to picture bureaucratic ideas of the art of government, he could desire no more apt example than Lord Curzon. And this for more than one reason. In the first place, under his ægis, bureaucracy in India reached the zenith of its development and most vividly exemplified the merits, the failings, the successes, the blunders, and the limitations of this form of government. From the epoch of the old autocratic rule until the commencement of this century, the machine of government had continued to grow in complexity and in efficiency until it attained, *as a machine*, an almost clocklike perfection. Henceforth, unless the omens err, the movement is to other shores, more spacious lands. Again, most typical officials eschew publicity, preferring to work unseen and uncriticized by the masses. Lord Curzon never shrank from the limelight. Serenely reliant on his own wisdom and foresight, he took the public into his confidence and set forth his ideals of government with a singular frankness and lucidity. For this end his unrivalled powers of eloquence—an eloquence somewhat marred by a too constant intrusion of the first personal pronoun—served him as a veritable Excalibur. Never before in the history of India had the administration been informed with such vigour or its principles and objectives so clearly announced. It is not, of course, suggested that previous Viceroys had been themselves bureaucrats or had been as wax in the hands of the great officials. Though more than one was content to become "merely the gilded figurehead of a bureaucratic administration," others, such as Lord Ripon, stood for ideals abhorrent to officials, and strove against heavy odds to enforce their views. It is Lord Curzon's distinction that his Indian career in no essential altered his original bent. He came to India a bureaucrat ready-made, imbued to the finger-tips with all the ideals of that theory of government, and resolute to enforce them. It was not that the officials moulded him to their views; he impressed his own conceptions on the officials with all the force of his authority and the vigour of his mind. He presented them, so to speak, with their own idols, transmuted into a fine gold by the alchemy of his genius, burnished and glittering from the fire of his eloquence and his imagination. But they were the idols of a bureaucrat and nothing else.

It is true that this was not Lord Curzon's own conception of his viceroyalty; like the Russian Czars, he imagined himself a sort of benevolent despot. On more than one occasion he even uttered a warning against the danger of converting the Government of India into a bureaucracy. But his whole policy, his acts, his speeches, and his resolutions when in India gave the lie to this conception of himself. Zealously he laboured to perfect the official machine, overhauling it with a passionate care, scrapping unnecessary parts here, oiling and polishing it there, and ever adding new complexities to enable it to perform more accurately its work. Nothing in any department was too small to escape his attention. No engineer in a warship ever took more pride in the perfection of his machinery, or sacrificed himself more completely to secure its efficiency. Yet, with one exception, outside this departmental zeal, we find little trace or indication of the broader aspects of statesmanship, any conception of the people other than that of potters' clay to be moulded and shaped into desired forms by the interaction of intricate machinery. He has himself defined with admirable precision the objective of the true bureaucrat: "The utmost that any one Government or head of a Government can effect," he declared, "is to hand over the administrative machine to the next comer with all its parts intact and in good working order." It would be difficult to define more accurately in so many words the aim, the strait and narrow aim, of the true official, or to present a more vivid synopsis of his own administration. After this we are not surprised to learn that the "whole secret of administration" lies in picking out the best men and giving them their chance, or that "efficiency of administration is a synonym for the contentment of the governed." Alas for the vanity of human wisdom! So far from efficiency of administration, as understood by Lord Curzon, being synonymous with the contentment of the people, it has been followed by the worst outburst of disloyalty and of sedition that has overshadowed India since the days of the Mutiny. Not even Lord Milner's forecast of the results of self-government in South Africa has been more signally belied by the event.

In questions of departmental administration it goes without saying that Lord Curzon has achieved many reforms.

Report-writing before his advent had been carried to an extreme which clogged official work and straggled out in inordinate delays. To this defect, so characteristic of a bureaucratic Government, he applied a drastic pruning-knife, so that now the bluebooks, if somewhat bald, have become at least readable. The amendment of the leave rules mitigated the evils of too frequent transfers of officers. After careful and lengthy inquiry, far-reaching reforms were effected in the Police and Irrigation Departments, though at a heavy expense. The work of famine relief was still further systematised and refined to the point of complexity. In the matter of education, though countless bluebooks were written, though conferences were held and elaborate minutes penned, the results failed to give satisfaction. Higher education, it was averred with justice, remained more than ever under the heel of Government, whilst on the other hand but little advance was made in the provision of primary schools, the crying need of the country. Archæology, excise, land revenue, and many other matters, all received attention from this strenuous Viceroy, in some improvement in details being effected, in others more drastic alterations. Sometimes, indeed, the reforms ended only in increased centralisation and in the creation of new and lucrative posts for officials. But the saving grace of Lord Curzon's administration, the problem in regard to which he showed real statesmanship, was his frontier policy. Although inveigled by the military party into a somewhat discreditable adventure in Thibet, he otherwise kept the Army element amongst his advisers in its proper place. He refused to permit the soldier to usurp the functions of the statesman. His frontier policy on the bloodstained Afghan border was a brilliant success. In place of constant raid and counter-raid he substituted a condition of comparative peace; futile expenditure ceased, and whereas in the five years ending 1899 four and a half millions sterling were squandered in military operations, a quarter of a million only represented the bill during the seven years of his viceroyalty. The secret of this success, as Lord Curzon himself declared, lay in treating the tribesmen "as if they were men of like composition with ourselves." Had he but applied the same policy to his conduct of the internal affairs of India, in how different a sky would his sun have set! True, the native of India is no picturesque cut-throat like the dwellers in the Afghan marches, but he also is a human being like ourselves, responsive to the same spurs, angered by the same affronts.

No event of Lord Curzon's viceroyalty was more characteristic of the man or illustrates more clearly the spirit of the bureaucrat, than the partition of Bengal. We may dismiss as unproved the accusation that its mainspring lay in a Machiavellian design to abase the Hindu and to exalt the Mohammedan, conceived of as more loyal to the Government of India. "Causes," as old William of Occam remarked, "are not to be multiplied beyond need," and the reason officially given amply explains the genesis of this disastrous measure. This was, that the administration of Bengal had become so onerous and complex as to make the proper government of the province impossible for a single Lieutenant-Governor. To relieve this officer, and to secure a higher standard of efficiency and control, it was therefore decided to split the province in two, Bengal proper and Eastern Bengal, the capital of the one continuing at Calcutta and that of the other being fixed at Dacca.

The course taken lies open to two obvious objections. In the first place, granting that the work had become too heavy to be coped with by the existing official machinery, there is no reason why the difficulty might not have been met by the creation of a Council, on the members of which would devolve a large portion of the burden of control, by devising measures of decentralisation and by the extension of self-government. In the second place—and herein lies the gravamen of the offence—Bengal had become a nation, with a nation's hopes, ideals, and aspirations. You cannot sunder a people in two without wounding their patriotism to the quick. By such an act they see their ambitions for ever destroyed, all that has inspired them in the past, all that they had dreamed of future glory and grandeur. Of course such considerations leave a bureaucrat cold. Sufficient for him that the administration becomes more efficient. If in so doing a people is crushed, a nation's manhood dwarfed, such an incident, whilst regrettable in its way, will soon be more than atoned for by the smoother working and greater accuracy of the machine. The partition of Bengal, after working immeasurable evil and constituting a focus of sedition and race hatred throughout India, has been finally cancelled through the enlightened foresight of another statesman. Bitterness and rancour have faded away, the fires of sedition burn low. It stands now in history as a monument to show the extreme of folly of which officialdom, divorced from generous ideals, is capable, perhaps, too, as a bench-mark defining the high-flood level of Indian bureaucracy.

The same blindness to the larger forces making for the organic life of a nation marred Lord Curzon's selection of men to fill the higher posts under his control. The upper stratum of officials tended more and more to become purely English. Although with the constant accessions to the cadres of every department the total number of natives employed greatly increased, the barriers shutting them off from all posts of supervision and control became at the same time more impassable than ever. Lord Curzon expressed a naïve surprise at the attacks made on him on this ground. He simply selected, he said, the most efficient man for the post—"the whole thing was so obvious as scarcely to need explanation." In support of this view, he adduced a despatch of the Court of Directors, dated 1833, in which it is averred that the people of India can best be benefitted by good government, not by holding out means for official distinction. But much water has flowed down the

Ganges since 1833. The people have become more educated, more self-conscious, more assertive, more keenly sensible of the injury done to their self-respect by their relegation to meaner and inferior posts. The example of Japan has demonstrated to them that the assumed inferiority of Asiatics derives largely, not from heredity but from environment. Given a suitable education and upbringing, an Asiatic, they contend, may hold his own in most departments of business and affairs. To find themselves thus debarred in their own country from every important office outside judgeships appears to their modern minds an unmerited stigma and affront, and this they resent bitterly. "If you touch the self-respect of a person," said one speaker, "you touch what he values more than life itself." This exclusion from higher posts came to reinforce the unrest aroused by the partition of Bengal. Here, again, the engineer, absorbed in the smooth working of his glittering machinery, had steered the ship of State into perilous waters, which, with a little observation of the winds and currents at work, might have been avoided so easily. Small wonder that Lord Minto found "an accumulated popular discontent," or that Lord Morley was obliged subsequently to observe that "of recent years the doctrine of administrative efficiency has been pushed too far." A people can be killed by efficiency.

Most bureaucrats seem to require from the people they govern a sort of reverent respect—reverence for their supreme wisdom, respect for the admirable manner in which they conduct the affairs of the nation. They are shocked at the display of any feelings incongruous with this attitude. A nation, in their estimation, is best conceived of as a number of schoolboys working and playing happily under the supervision of benevolent and very wise schoolmasters. Individuals may have to be corrected from time to time, and may even become a little restive under necessary discipline, but in the long run they will revert to the traditional attitude of respect. Lord Curzon was no exception to this rule ; on the contrary, he admirably typified it. On more than one occasion, and in particular on a visit to Burma, he emphasized the advantages and the necessity of such an attitude towards rulers. Now, if there is one fault which the Burman has, it is an excessive veneration for authority, a deference to officials as officials, and a distrust of his own initiative and judgment. To harp, then, on this virtue of reverence—so convenient to the rulers—was in effect to gild the lily, or to urge frugality on the Spartans. A wise orator, one who really desired the advancement of the race, would have rather extolled the virtues that spring from a virile independence of opinion. But those are the last virtues that find favour in the eyes of a bureaucrat.

That it was from no apprehension of hurting the feelings of the Burmese that Lord Curzon so framed his discourse is clear from his too famous homily in February, 1905, at the Convocation of Calcutta University. To an audience composed of the most intellectual elements of

Bengali society he declared that their besetting sin lay in a certain tendency to—well, let us say, to embroider the facts, and he expatiated with much unction on the virtues of truthfulness. Now, whether inveracity is or is not a fault of the Bengali, it would be difficult to conceive a grosser instance of want of tact, or an utterance more calculated to fan to white heat the fire of racial hatred. It was nothing to the point to quote a Bengali paper on the relatively low standard of truthfulness in India. It is one thing to be criticized by one's fellow-countrymen and quite another to be criticized by a foreigner. No self-respecting people will brook from the latter humiliating aspersions on their race which expose them to contempt or derision. Imagine, for instance, the French Ambassador, in an address after some unsuccessful war, supporting an accusation of cowardice against the English people by an excerpt from an English newspaper. The country would rise up like one man and rend him.

The egregious folly of Lord Curzon's

remarks can best be explained on the supposition that he considered himself in the light of a benevolent headmaster dealing faithfully for their own good with the faults of a class of pupils. This attitude, quite characteristic of him, would alone account for his walking wide-eyed into so obvious a pitfall. In such a view he might conceive of his hearers as receiving, with much searching of heart and a humble resolve for amendment, the strictures which he felt it his painful duty to convey. That would only be befitting of little boys, and particularly of good little boys who held their teacher in proper reverence. Unfortunately, grown men, with the passions of men, proud of their race and sensitive for its honour, do not see criticisms in quite the same light. The storm of indignation and anger roused by the words of Lord Curzon indicated how deeply he had wounded the sensitive natives of India, and how completely he had failed to gauge the real forces that inspire the cultured classes in that country.

Hardly less wide of the mark was his

appeal on the same occasion for a temperate and suggestive—not hostile—public opinion, which was to be representative of native sentiment generally and not of one section of it. Such a public opinion deferentially brought to the notice of Government—very much as a number of nice little boys with Eton jackets and white collars might make a suggestion to their headmaster—would, no doubt, be entirely consonant with the ideals of an enlightened bureaucrat. It would gently stimulate him without the introduction of any rude or jarring element. But, outside a comic opera, no more impossible dream was ever dreamed.

Native opinion, like the opinion of all countries touched by modern thought, is reft into two classes with conflicting and irreconcilable ideals. The one, *enfants de la tradition*, sets before everything the upholding of order and authority; the evolution of society along the forms hallowed by long usage; a progress orderly and not too precipitate of the lower classes through the influence of Government and the historic leaders of the people. The other, *enfants de l'esprit nouveau*, aspires to a renovation of society by the act of the people themselves, who must therefore, before all things, be widely educated ; they cherish patriotic aims ; they disdain foreign help and strive towards a vigorous, self-governing organism, quickened by high ideals and pulsating with national life. The cold formality of bureaucratic government chills such reformers ; its inertia exasperates them ; they break their hearts against the barriers it opposes to popular control and popular progress. Whatever be the case with the first school of thought, it were idle to expect from the second a decorous submission to authority. The first may be compared to a placid lake, the second to a foaming mountain torrent, which, according to the course it takes, may bring blessings on the country or convulse it by disaster, but which will never, from its nature, pour down in a tranquil and well-regulated stream.

The suggestion, made in England, for

the removal of questions affecting the government of India from the sphere of party politics strikes the same chord of thought. Such a notion has haunted other minds besides Lord Curzon's. We have seen the same plausible proposal put forward by politicians in respect to foreign policy, in respect to education, in respect to the Army. The speaker suggests that the great department in question should be "elevated" above the dust of party strife, into some serene and pure atmosphere, where experts like archangels move, and where questions are decided, not through the ebb and flow of wrangling forces but according to the dictates of pure reason. In this refined ether alone shall we grasp that Holy Grail, a continuity of policy. But what policy is it that shall be continued? Which of the two great schools of thought shall receive the crown? shall be chosen to stamp its conceptions for ever on the conduct of a great department of Government? These ideals clash irrevocably, and no half-way course between them is practicable, nor can endure for long. If some Ministers dream of a policy in which the blandness of the Conservative oil will blend pleasantly with the acidity of the Liberal lemon, they will soon be disillusioned. Not thus do men conduct their affairs in a world of strife. Continuity of foreign policy, for instance, in these latter days has, in the opinion of many, meant continuity of Conservative foreign policy. One would search in vain in recent years for traces of that ethical right, that respect for weak nationalities, and that support of the oppressed which formed the cardinal features of Liberalism under Gladstone. Machiavelli has usurped the throne of Christ. So in India, when Lord Curzon pleaded for continuity of policy he obviously had in his mind a perpetual government according to Conservative conceptions. That form of government has its merits, but they are merits which, in the opinion of Liberals, are eclipsed by its inherent defects. Rightly or wrongly, Liberals conceive it to be stunted and narrow, and unsuited for the requirements of an India that has begun to move. And in practice also continuity of policy connotes increased power and control by the permanent officials. The more you set up this fetish of continuity the more you fall under the influence of office routine and office tradition, the less amenable does the helmsman become to the generous currents of opinion, whether of one party or the other, which sway the minds of plain men in a free country.

But why this shunning of party conflict? Does not all progress, whether in nature or in the intellect, spring from mutual strife? and is not orthodoxy or uniformity of opinion just a synonym for stagnation? The one is life, organic growth; the other the hardening of arteries that forebodes decay. After all, as Bismarck remarked, "*nur die Konflickte nicht zu tragisch nehmen.*" There is no need to wring one's hands over the spectacle of men arrayed in warring camps. Let us rather rejoice that men are still touched to the quick by questions affecting the government of themselves and of others, that they are still moved by great ideals which, whether on the one side or the other, contain much that is noble, generous, and inspiring.

In his relations with the various members of his Council, Lord Curzon enjoyed, as he himself relates, the unique advantage of an almost unbroken harmony. Indeed, he is at pains to contrast the unanimity that prevailed during his viceroyalty with the discords and opposition against which his predecessors had frequently to struggle. But does not this very unanimity, this harmonious concord, tell its own tale? Surely it was because Lord Curzon saw eye to eye with Indian officials, and because in all questions of policy his views coincided with theirs. Men will not be found to agree for years at a time on a multiplicity of questions unless the views they hold on fundamentals are practically identical. If, for instance, Mr. Lloyd George were to preside over a Conservative Cabinet, trouble, and serious trouble, would not be long delayed. It is not as though the Members of Council yield a willing deference to the Viceroy, and acquiesce tamely in his views. On the contrary, they have never hesitated to express frankly their own views in complete independence of those of their nominal head. Lord Ripon realized this to his cost on more than one occasion. In 1862 we have Lord Elgin writing that he had actually less power as Viceroy of India than as Governor of Canada with a free Parliament. Clearly, then, the unanimity in Lord Curzon's time sprang from no tame subservience to the views of a strenuous ruler, but from an unfeigned agreement on the principles and objectives which should direct the Government. Officials found in him a kindred spirit; bureaucrats, the archetype of a bureaucrat. No wonder that a peace as of Eden reigned within the walls of the Council Chamber!

In the eternal irony of human affairs few events strike one more forcibly than the grim aftermath of sedition and crime that darkened the termination of his rule. He brought so much energy, ability, and zeal to the discharge of his task; he laboured so strenuously for the welfare of the governed, this Viceroy who held sway fifty years too late. Surely you would say this devotion to the duties of his post would have kindled a glow of affection in the masses whose welfare he held so much at heart. Such an outcome he himself fully anticipated. On more than one occasion he asserted with confidence that loyalty had been strengthened through his administrative reforms; he even expected Bengalis to bless him one day for the partition of their country. "It is by native confidence in British justice," he cried, "that the loyalty of the Indian people is assured." Now, if there was one thing on which Lord Curzon prided himself—as he has been at some pains to explain—it was his sense of justice, so that if this dictum held true he should have received a rich guerdon of love and gratitude. But the time was long overpast when a merely just government would have satisfied the aspirations of the Indian people. They would prefer a just bureaucrat to an unjust bureaucrat —indeed, have not most English rulers in

India been just?—but that is not enough. A people hungering for self-government will not be placated by good government, however intricate, however conscientious, however benevolent. Not thus can you quench the fires of patriotism, or efface the stigma with which men shut off from high posts, debarred from all power of self-government, feel themselves branded before the face of Asia. They asked for bread, and Lord Curzon gave them a stone. Neither the nobility of his ideas nor the eloquence with which he clothed them availed one iota to atone for this cardinal blunder of his administration. It was through this blindness to the living realities of an organic growth, this rigid outlook, that his tenure of office, which dawned with such roseate promise of success, ended in a depressing sense of failure, a failure that narrowly escaped becoming a disaster.

PROVINCIAL GOVERNMENT

CHAPTER V

PROVINCIAL GOVERNMENT

THE selection of a province of India to illustrate the working of the bureaucratic system presents certain obvious difficulties. No two are alike. They differ one from another in history, whether under native or English rule, in geographic circumstances, in race, in culture, in religion, and in economic development. The disparity between England and Spain is not less than that between the Punjab and Madras; religious rancour sunders Mohammedan from Hindu as effectually as Roman Catholic from Protestant. But though India, like Europe, presents a hundred diversities of nations and tribes, there is, as in Europe, an underlying similarity in thought which sets its hall-mark on the masses, and differentiates them as a whole from other sections of the human race. The term "Indian" connotes certain definite attributes. And India has what Europe has not, a central Government which rules on uniform principles, and which, in fact, prides itself on the uniformity of its rule. In mere point of governance, therefore, much that obtains in one province will hold good, too, of others. One province may rear a more stately edifice of government or may hold by more modern and advanced ideals, but the materials and the general plan will be much the same.

Burma may at first blush seem somewhat unsuitable as an example of Indian provincial government. Geographically, it lies apart from the rest of India, whilst the Mongolian race and the Buddhist religion number but a small fraction of the millions of India proper. Nevertheless, it possesses more than countervailing advantages. By the homogeneity of its people and its religion, those manifold complexities and reservations that distract in India are wholly avoided; the questions of government become relatively simple. Religious bitternesses scarcely exist, for the gentle tolerance of Buddhism creates an atmosphere inimical to them. Nor does the structure of Burmese society permit the growth of that powerful aristocracy which introduces so picturesque but disturbing an element in Indian affairs. In nature the Burmese are docile, obedient to authority, and kindly, presenting an ideally plastic material to the hand of the bureaucratic potter. In no part of India have the conquerors possessed a freer hand to mould a people according to their ideals, and to guide their steps towards a higher civilization. Here has history proffered to the English rulers a *tabula rasa* whereon they may inscribe the growth of a race as they would have it grow. If to these considerations we add the fact of the comparatively recent annexation of the lower and upper provinces, thus precluding traditions bequeathed from the old autocratic days of the East India Company, it will be admitted that for the purpose of a conspectus of bureaucratic government the province is not without its advantages.

For some little time after the seizure of a country by force of arms, military or autocratic methods will naturally find favour in the councils of Government. The new rulers fear before everything risings having for object the subversion of their still raw authority, as yet unmellowed by the influence of time and tradition. To the paramount necessity of holding the subject race in check and of preserving peace among men still seething with discontent, every other consideration must bow. It was not until some twenty years after the incorporation of Lower Burma in the Indian Empire that autocracy in Lower Burma began to crystallize into a bureaucratic system. When the process was yet inchoate, the annexation of Upper Burma in 1883, and the resulting widespread disturbances, shattered for the time secretariat control, and made imperative a return to more primitive methods.

This event, by the way, possesses two

points of more than merely local interest. In the first place, the *casus belli* was curiously parallel with that which sixteen years later cost England untold millions in South Africa. In each case Government was influenced in its decision by powerful financial interests operating in a foreign country, in Burma by the Bombay Burman Trading Company, in the Transvaal by the Rand lords. In each case those interests, to add weight to their representations, set up the bogey of foreign intrigue — in Burma by France, in the Transvaal by Germany—both allegations subsequently being proved exaggerated. Many people now consider the grievances of the mining companies to have been grossly overstated, and there was excellent justification for the fine levied by the King of Burma on the Bombay Company for malpractices in the forests. Thus do financiers pervert to their will high-minded statesmen, and sway the destiny of nations.

In the second place, the prolonged disturbances and numerous risings which followed the annexation revealed a quite unsuspected depth of patriotism amongst the Burmese. When a loosely knit, half-civilized nation has been subjugated with no great battles or slaughter of men, the conquerors may usually expect serious trouble in the course of the next few years. The people have not felt the real weight of the victor's hand, and, ignorant as they are of the realities of armaments, they struggle futilely, like birds caught in a cage, to release themselves from its grip. And the extent and gravity of the disturbances, which involved Lower as well as Upper Burma, came as a surprise to even experienced officers. They had not realized that under a docile and courteous demeanour the Burmese cherish a well-spring of ardent patriotism, or, as Lord Randolph Churchill styled it in a dispatch, of "national vanity." (An Englishman, by the way, who has not some "national vanity" is thought a rather poor sort of creature.) The blotting out of their race from the roll of independent nations wounded them to the quick. Said one of them with bitterness: "We have no longer a king; you have made us like the *Kulas*" (natives of India). The anguish of outraged patriotism welled up in a roaring surge of rebellion and brigandage which in a moment swept over the land, sapped the foundations of order and of civil life, and only ebbed after years of strife and misery. However base and cruel the acts of many leaders of bands, however much those outlaws were imbued with the spirit of sheer plunder, undoubtedly the mainspring of their dogged resistance was patriotism, and nothing else. Like a shaft of sunlight athwart a rain-swept landscape, this fact redeems much that was cruel, base, pathetically futile, and throws over the history of a thousand petty conflicts some element of moral grandeur. It was the tragedy of a shackled nation, impotently struggling to be free. Let us learn from it the depth and height and strength of patriotic fire which the impassivity of an Oriental may conceal but does not slake.

The means by which the pacification of Burma was eventually accomplished were threefold. The country was completely disarmed. Many thousand men of the warlike races of the north-west of India were brought over and formed into a military police. A drastic village law enforced collective responsibility on the peasantry and strengthened the position of the headman, the agent of Government in the village. The last two measures demand some particular mention. The military police is a body which was and is organized under military officers who, in Upper Burma, are responsible for its discipline and internal economy. In Lower Burma the district superintendents of police control it with the assistance of adjutants. It has no detective duties, its function consisting in the provision of guards, the garrisoning of the hill tracts, and the destruction of outlaw bands where these exist. Owing to the high rates of pay authorized both for the officers and men, the military police force constitutes a very formidable item in the Provincial Budget. The Village Act requires the inhabitants of a village to resist dacoits, to arrest murderers, robbers, and certain other offenders, and to give up stolen property tracked to their boundary.[1] Failure to comply with these provisions entails a fine on the whole village. The headman, besides being endowed with petty magisterial and civil authority, is authorized to enforce from the villagers the multitudinous duties enjoined on them by the law. These include measures of sanitation, the construction and repair of roads or of stockades, the despatch of official letters, keeping watch at night, the reporting of the arrival of visitors, the provision of transport for officials or labour for public works. All these services except the last must be performed without remuneration. In addition to these duties the headman collects the revenue, for which he receives a commission, and assists generally in the prevention and detection of crime. It will be admitted that this village law, if

[1] Compare the law of Khammurabi: "If the robber is not caught . . . the town and its governor within the limits of which the robbery took place shall give back to him everything he has lost."

vigorously worked—and it has been very vigorously worked—constitutes a most potent weapon for the pacification of a country and for the despatch at a minimum of cost of many of the minor functions of government.

By these means and the strenuous exertions of its officers the Burma Government succeeded early in the nineties in quelling the disturbances and in establishing a standard of security which the country certainly did not possess under its native rulers. Officials and travellers could move about everywhere in safety; the honest trader or peasant possessed his goods in peace. Ardent reformers, particularly those of the extreme left, such as our Socialist or anarchist friends, are somewhat apt to under-estimate the sovereign importance of this security of property. Only those who have witnessed the calamities that flow from insecurity, its paralysing effects on industry, trade, and the whole life of a country can realize how much is involved in the maintenance of law and order. Probably a taste of real anarchy would effectually cure most philosophic anarchists. Evils, gross evils no doubt, spring up and flourish under the protection of the law as fungi under the swelling arch of an oak, but they do not compare with the evils which a dissolution of social order must bring in its train. If to the uncertainties of the seasons, the vicissitudes of trade, the thousand and one mischances which bring to naught the best endeavours of men, you superadd the seizure of their hard-won gains by acts of violence, you take from them the last incentive to exertion. Men are all, as Emerson remarked, as lazy as they dare; diligence implies a strong incentive to goad or to lure. Unless a people has a reasonable certainty of reaping what it has sown trade will decline and tilth draw in her borders. In the conferment of the blessings of peace on Burma, equally with India, the British Government has deserved well of the people, and has earned a meed of gratitude which should not be forgotten in any outcry against its shortcomings.

Closely allied to this security against acts of violence is the protection from cheating and injustice afforded by the institution of upright courts of law. Under the native regime justice wore an uncertain mien, and the scales were too often weighted in favour of the wealthier and more unscrupulous litigant. These defects to some extent remain under the British system, which errs, too, on the side of complexity, but on the whole the present administration of civil justice vastly excels that of former days. To these kindred boons of order and justice may be added that of good communications by rail or road—by river, security alone suffices to multiply the traffic a hundred-fold. Order, justice, and roads—that is the trinity which support the material prosperity of a country; and it is precisely on these objects that the English in Burma, as in India, have bent their energies, and which they have emblazoned on their banner as the insignia of a really good Government. In so doing they have but unconsciously followed in the steps of those Roman proconsuls who, nearly two thousand years ago, ruled under the Roman eagles over such diverse peoples in the ancient world. And in so far as their horizon has been limited to these three objectives they have been rewarded by the Roman measure of success.

On the annexation of Lower Burma the English found in existence a capitation or poll tax levied on each adult male, with a double rate for those who had renounced single blessedness. Exceptions existed in the case of certain classes, such as paupers, monks, and—significantly enough —Government officials. This tax they have continued to the present day, maintaining, as might be anticipated, the exceptions. As already stated, it is a tax which is wholly unknown in India. But it happened to be in existence at the time of the conquest of Lower Burma, and, true to their tradition to alter institutions of native origin as little as possible—particularly when these conduce to their pecuniary advantage—the English incorporated the tax into their system. Not the morality, still less the statesmanship, of such a tax has ever been seriously discussed; that the people were accustomed to it has been deemed a sufficient and adequate justification.

Similarly after the annexation of Upper Burma there has been continued the *Thathameda*, literally a tax of ten rupees per house. As a matter of fact, the tax was of quite recent origin, taking the place of a levy of tribute, village by village, by former kings. Nor could any good reason be alleged why two entirely different systems of taxation should sunder Lower from Upper Burma. Yet the Government of India ruled otherwise, and sanctioned this anomaly as well as the continuance in practice of a singularly uneven and archaic method of taxation.

It need not, however, be supposed that, in adopting the old system our thrifty Government has been content with the moderate returns which satisfied the Burmese kings. The latter, when fixing the rates of taxation, knew well that, partly through the laxity of subordinates, partly through corruption, a large proportion of the nominal revenue would never leave the pockets of their subjects. It may, indeed, be argued that both in Burma and in India the native rulers, bearing this fact in mind, fixed rates of taxation which to some will appear severe, if not harsh. It was not the nominal rate so much as the actual incidence which they would consider. Be this as it may, the new rulers had no compunction as to the equity of collecting to the utmost farthing the taxes first imposed at the hands of the Burmese kings. Sufficient for them that the impost had been collected, with whatever shortcomings or laxity, by the native rulers whom they superseded. A well-known Indian judge once exclaimed that he was there to administer, not justice but the law; even so in matters of taxation it has not been the equity of an impost, but its legality, which forms the major premise in each proposition. With the improved organization and closer check on subordinates even the dullest farmer and labourer has begun to understand all that is implied in "the strict letter of the law," and that under the sky and on this earth—to borrow a Chinese phrase—there is no escape from the dues which Government, in its wisdom, demands from its loyal subjects. Levied lightly and with many omissions in the early years of our government, the assessment and collection of the revenue has with improved organization tended more and more to mechanical perfection. If there is one department of its activities of which a bureaucracy may legitimately boast itself, in which it triumphs over other forms of government, it is in the strict collection of its legal dues. The Burma Government, equally with other provincial Governments of India, is entitled to all the credit that is due to supreme efficiency in this respect. Only—and this is important—let not its apologists assert that it has in no wise added to the people's burdens, for this is not true. In letter only the incidence remains unaltered; in practice it has notably increased.

It might have been supposed that, with

the pacification of the country, the Village Act, with its drastic and exceptional provisions, would have been sensibly modified to meet the altered conditions. A good horseman does not ride a docile steed on the curb. But those who think thus do not know the soul of a bureaucracy. No bureaucracy will voluntarily abdicate powers, however irksome, to the common people, which conduce to the convenience of officials, or which strengthen their grip upon the country. In the case of the Village Act, so comprehensive are the powers conferred that it is no exaggeration to say that it places the entire population in the hands of the district officers. Is labour required for Public Works or any other Government department? The villagers must supply it. Does an official require carts or provisions? They must be promptly tendered. Do the police, through inefficiency, fail to arrest a criminal or permit the countryside to be infested by outlaws? The villagers may be fined, forced to beat the jungles, or keep watch year in year out. They must repair free of cost the roads near the village, maintain the village stockade when there is one—stockades were continued long after there was any necessity—keep the village in a sanitary condition, assist in the collection of revenue, and report to the headman the name of every arrival, and to district officials a thousand and one matters which officialdom likes to know. In all things they must obey their headman, himself the servant of higher officials. It would be difficult to conceive any enactment framed by the wit of man more calculated to crush out the life and spirit of a people, and to reduce them to the status of humble, tractable servants of the official hierarchy. Village administration, far from forming a school for local self-government, seems in danger of conversion into a branch of the bureaucracy.

But even this Act failed to satisfy the official craving for power—after all, appetite grows in eating. Accordingly, in 1907, on a revision of the law, it was enacted that no person can establish a new village without the permission of the district officer, the ostensible reason being to prevent criminals living in isolated huts. Criminals do not, however, live in isolated huts, but in large centres of population, and in any case the reason given was utterly inadequate. Since no person may take up his residence in an existing village without the permission of the headman, it will be admitted the Government have, in theory at least, established a fairly complete control over the lives of their subjects. One fetter only is lacking—the Russian system of passports.

The corvées—they are euphemistically termed "free" labour—constitute, like those in pre-revolutionary France, no light tax on the peasantry. Apart from the duty of carrying messages or letters, the time occupied in repairing stockades or in maintaining roads is quite considerable. In respect to roads, whilst at first the village had only to maintain that between their village and the nearest police-post, it must now, under the Act of 1907, maintain all roads between itself and the neighbouring villages, however distant these may be. And occasionally these corvées may entail rather dire consequences. It is on record that in the Minbu district villagers were forced to labour without pay at the canal headworks in malarious tracts, and that in consequence several of them died.

As with the drastic provisions of the Village Act, so with the other instrument of pacification; the military police continued practically at war strength long after any real need for so great a force had ceased. This body of men is unavailable for ordinary police duties, and is extremely costly to maintain. Obvious reasons of policy would deprecate the policing of a country by men alien in race, in language, and in creed. But, as already pointed out, a bureaucracy, conscious that it has not the real gratitude and loyalty of the governed, is ever apprehensive for its own security. There are always, it reflects, so many who fail to appraise its service at their true value, who cherish absurd ideas of "national vanity." With the entire control of the purse-strings, it takes care, therefore, whilst scrimping the expenditure on other departments, to give with both hands to the chiefs of internal defence. Thus in 1909-10 the total expenditure on the police in Burma amounted to 117 lacs of rupees out of a provincial expenditure of 433 lacs. In other words, considerably more than a fourth of the available revenues was expended on the police-force alone—this, too, in addition to a liberal force of regular troops maintained by the Imperial Government and amongst a population wholly disarmed. No wonder the development of the young and prosperous province is delayed and trammelled by want of funds, no wonder the urgent demands for more schools and roads remain unsatisfied! The military police may truly be said to hang like a millstone round the neck of Burma.

In spite of ample regular troops, in spite of serried ranks of military police, the conduct of the Government has often evinced an apprehensive timidity in cases where one might well expect boldness and resolution. The cultivation of the poppy in

Burma is contrary to our declared policy, yet no serious attempt has been made to stamp it out amongst the Kachins in the north. Not only so, but when of recent years a scarcity of opium has ensued from the suppression of poppy cultivation in China, an actual increase in the area in Burma has been chronicled. Could any contrast be more humiliating to patriotic Englishmen? On the one side, China, feeble in military force, with exiguous railways and wretched roads, racked by internal dissension, yet daring all for the suppression of the national curse; on the other, Burma, with a stable Government, an overwhelming military force, and a comparatively excellent system of communications, fearing to lift up her little finger to eradicate the poppy amongst a handful of ill-armed hillmen. But China is inspired by a passionate desire for the regeneration and the progress of her people.

Again, most Englishmen cherish the illusion that the Union Jack flies only over the free, that under our rule slavery exists but as an evil and half-forgotten dream. A slave, they think, has only to tread the sacred soil of our Empire and his fetters drop from off him. Yet to this day the Kachin chiefs possess slaves, and the status of these slaves is officially recognized by our Government. For these unfortunates at least the English flag does not spell liberty. The change of Government has for them no meaning; for them the might of the British Empire, its armies, its police, the pomp and ordered strength of its rulers is as though it had never been. A bureaucratic Government, boasting of its efficiency and its enlightenment, has not dared to lift up its head to these chiefs and say, "Your slaves are free."

Turning to the question of education in Burma, we are confronted by an unwonted—unwonted, that is, in India—and interesting system. It has ever been the pious and laudable rule of the monastic order in that country that they should teach the boys of the village the elements of reading and writing, and instil in them precepts proper for wayfarers along the Noble Path. This education, it should be remembered, is given free of charge, for no Buddhist monk may touch a piece of money. Accordingly, in all monasteries—and each village has its monastery—a certain portion of time is set aside for the instruction of the young. No sight is more familiar than the groups of young urchins seated cross-legged on the spacious floors of these buildings, reciting texts after the Oriental manner at the top of their voices or writing studiously on black parchment, under the supervision of a reverend brother of the yellow robe. This system, so native to the soil, the English Government has, not unnaturally, attempted to foster and to develop. It is hallowed by long custom, it has all the people's love, it costs nothing, and last, but not least, it inculcates, or is believed to inculcate, docility and subservience to authority. But it possesses two incurable defects. In the first place, the vast majority of the monks are not educationists; they don the yellow robe for the purpose of their holy religion and inspired by its truths, and they view askance both the scope and methods of modern education. Geography many frankly refuse to teach, since it clashes with the dogmas of Buddhism. In the second place, the object of their instruction is purely religious. Secular subjects find in it only a minor and subordinate place. These defects are radical; they inhibit any conversion of the monastic system of education into one with reasonable claims to efficiency. You might as well endeavour by cultivation to transform a lily into an apple-tree as seek to develop this indigenous system on true educational lines. The thing will not work. But the fact will never be recognized by the Burma Government, even in those fleeting moments when, amidst its other abstractions, it finds time to cast a hasty glance at the progress or otherwise of education. Because the monastic schools inculcate docility—like monastic schools in all countries—because they are cheap they will ever be beloved by a bureaucratic Government. *It is not education so much as docility that officials desire*. Education, properly so called, means the development of a people by themselves, on their own free lines, not a development supervised and controlled by officials. And to your true official all that is anathema.

One of the best tests of the value of an educational system is the volume of crime in the country, or portion of the country, under its influence. Thus in England, with efficient schools, we have half-empty prisons. North Italy, with its schools and enlightenment, contrasts sharply with the ignorant and murder-ridden south. Bombay and Madras, the two most progressive provinces in India, have also the best jail record. Thanks to the smattering of reading and writing taught in the monasteries, Burma ranks highest amongst the Indian provinces in the percentage of "literates," a fact often adduced by obscurantists by way of support to a policy of inaction. Yet the total number of convicts, in spite of its scanty population, is nearly the same as in populous Madras, and exceeds those of Bombay and the Punjab. No wonder the Burmese jails are overcrowded. It is interesting to note that the proportion of literates among the convicts is thrice that of Madras, the next highest province. What sort of education is this, what claim has it to support or countenance, that so signally fails to control crime and to evolve law-abiding citizens?

Certainly the amount of money expended on the schools has not been excessive. In 1889-90, out of a total expenditure of 185 lacs, in Lower Burma, under 4 lacs, or less than 2 per cent., went to their support. Ten years later the proportion was about the same—that is to say, for the entire province, 7 lacs out of about 300. In 1909-10, with a provincial expenditure of 433 lacs, education claimed 19 lacs, or about 5 per cent. The true significance of these figures will be apparent when one remembers that this provincial total excludes expenditure on the Army or railways, and that in the same year 117 lacs were lavished on the police. This, then, is the measure of the interest which a bureaucratic Government takes in the education of its subjects! The people perish for lack of light, but officialdom stares at their misery with blind, unseeing eyes. Russia might so govern, Turkey might so govern, England might have so governed a century ago; but that English rulers in this twentieth century should thus misuse the powers committed to them must bring a blush to the cheek of every lover of his country. Contrast the vigorous and living educational movement amongst the Chinese with the deathlike torpor in Burma. It is not that the Burmese are averse to good education, or fail to support the exiguous modern schools scattered throughout the land. On the contrary, they passionately desire a really sound education for their children, if only such were placed within their reach. It is the sinister figure of bureaucracy that bars the way, wedded to an obsolete system, indifferent or hostile to any real enlightenment of the people.

Two paths were open to our Government

when the turmoils of the conquest had died away: the path of repression, of manacles and whips and barriers, of ruling the vanquished country with the sword ever at her throat; and the path of conciliation by an appeal to her best and highest aspirations, by leading her, hand-in-hand, through the dark opposing valleys up towards the light. Alas! the way chosen has been the iron way of military force. For Burma, England still stands a menacing conqueror, armed to the teeth, not a torch-bearer of knowledge, a kindly guide to a higher civilization. The pity of it all! So superb, so incomparably free and untrammelled was the work of redemption that lay ready to our hands, so halting and pitiable has been the performance. Will a bureaucracy ever learn that mechanical accuracy is not life, that a drilled automaton is no substitute for the life and spirit of a living organism?

Lord Curzon once humorously remarked, by way of deprecating the influence he was popularly supposed to exert, that a sparrow could scarcely twitter its tail in Peshawar without men discerning in it the hand of the masterful Viceroy. But in truth the influence exerted by a bureaucratic head is very real. Provincial governors, themselves arch-bureaucrats, hail with avidity ideas in harmony with their own when enunciated with all the authority that hedges the regent of the King; they can now give full reign to their secret inclinations, from which the last checks are removed. Certainly this was the case in Burma. The Lieutenant-Governor of the province under Lord Curzon was Sir Herbert White, a typical Secretariat-trained official, of exceptional ability and kindly presence, but marred by the limitations insuperable from his up-bringing. His tenure of office was signalized, not only by the retrograde Village Act already noted, but by an abortive Bill to render the villagers responsible for the defalcations of their headman. The avowed object of this unjust measure was to save officials the trouble of taking security. Other legislation, happily equally abortive, was framed with a view to amend the law relating to landlord and tenant and to restrict alienation of land. Both these matters cried aloud for redress, but when the pivot of the suggested reform is, not the ordered precedent of the Law Courts but the arbitrary fiat of the district officer, it may well be that the remedy would prove worse than the disease. It is only by substituting the supremacy of the law for the will of individuals that we really advance. What certainty of contract, what confidence or stability could farmers possess, when all hangs threadlike on the whim of an overworked official? The latter's benevolence of intention and unquestioned probity in no way counterbalance the inherent vice of such a system, which, if adopted, would have proved as unworkable in practice as it was reactionary in principle. Other measures, such as the increased subordination of municipalities to district officers, testified to the growing intensification of bureaucratic control.

But perhaps it was in his speeches that

Sir Herbert White displayed most clearly his characteristic bias, and betrayed the influence of Lord Curzon. "The final aim and object of government," he declared at Mandalay, "is to assure to the trader, the farmer, and the artisan, the safe and free pursuit of their several callings, to all men security and equal justice, and full opportunity of making moral and material progress." Government is here conceived of as overarching and protecting the people, as the blue sky covers and shields us from the naked cold of space, but wholly dissevered from them, and forming an entity in which they have no part or lot. With such a government you may have material prosperity, but you will not have "moral progress"—if indeed that shibboleth of the Indian Government means anything more than empty words. If you deprive a nation of all share in its own government, in the forging of its destiny, you emasculate its energies, undermine its character, and sear, as with a hot iron, its self-respect. In the sphere of the intellect such a government spells, not progress but decay.

Amongst a people so accursed it is idle to look for those great moral enthusiasms which in happier countries have transfigured whole peoples, gleaming as beacon lights to guide the march of their advance. The nation sinks into a kind of spiritless torpor. In vain did Sir Herbert White again and again adjure his listeners to hearken to their elders and suppress the opium habit, the bane of Burma. "It is for the people themselves," he declared, "to see that the mischief of opium is remedied." Most excellent precept! But why should they try to please the fair eyes of an alien Government? How can they strive when sedulously deprived of all power and initiative? It is not men treated as little children, repressed as little children, who achieve these reformations, but free citizens, responsible and therefore zealous for the fair fame of their country.

But to a bureaucrat the power and virtue of true patriotism must ever remain a sealed book. Here is an instance. In reference to the annexation of Upper Burma, the Lieutenant-Governor once gravely informed the natives of that country that "Burma as a whole acquired the proud privilege of becoming a part of the British Empire." There is no reason to suppose that in uttering this *bétise* he was aiming a sardonic taunt at a conquered people; it merely signalizes the total ignorance of human feelings that marks the true bureaucrat, particularly the Imperialist variety of the species. You have conquered us, and you have cut us off from amongst the nations, and have humbled us into the dust, and yet you expect us to be proud of the fact. Imagine some strong and prosperous mediæval baron seizing a peasant living on the borders of his domain, and saying to him: "You will now form one of my establishment. You will be fed and cared for; in fact, you will be introduced to all the luxuries of civilization. If you are docile and obedient to me, we shall get on rarely together. You may, indeed, be proud of numbering yourself amongst my retainers." "True," would rejoin the peasant, "I am in material respects more comfortable. But before I was my own master, free to live my own life, free to look the whole world in the face, proud of my race and my freedom. It is not the same."

In his attitude towards the spiritual development of the people Sir Herbert White represented, one fears, only too accurately that of bureaucrats in general. They "remember only that man has property and forget that he has a soul." To a superficial observer, China, with its tottering Government, its foot-tracks doing duty as roads, and its faulty system of justice, may appear to be, as compared with Burma, in the dark ages. Yet China possesses what Burma has not, the priceless gift of a living national spirit, an ardent fire of patriotism. As a racehorse surpasses a driven hack, so may she in the long run excel Burma, not only in mental development, but also in material progress. Already in the two vital questions of opium and education she bids fair to put to the blush all our boasted efficacy of administration. If this should ever come to pass, if China should evolve a superior civilization to that attained under our rule, then will England stand at the bar of Asia convicted, in spite of her protestations, of degrading where she should have exalted, of the betrayal of those confided to her care, whom it was her bounden duty to educate, and to establish as a vigorous and progressive people.

TOWARDS DEMOCRACY

CHAPTER VI

TOWARDS DEMOCRACY

A DISTINGUISHED anthropologist has pointed out that even superstitions which we now all ridicule or condemn, have in certain times contributed in no small measure to the stability of human society. Thus the idea of taboo has fortified the Polynesian islanders' respect for private property; and in diverse countries many a would-be murderer has recoiled from the deed from fear of the vengeance of a malignant ghost. So, too, with Governments. Forms of government gravely defective in principle or pernicious in their moral effect on the people may yet act beneficially, nay, be indispensable, in certain stages of the political development of a nation. That is a proposition which even the extremist Radical would scarcely be concerned to deny. You could not establish with any hope of success parliamentary institutions amongst the Waganda. In South America democracy would seem to have been embraced with a too hasty enthusiasm, though in parts even of that continent there are signs of ultimate success.

Bureaucratic government may be said to find its true function in the provision of a kind of training school to bridge over the gap between autocracy on the one hand and some form of popular government on the other, to form a nexus, as it were, between the barbaric pomp of the mediæval monarch and the sober institutions that characterize democracy. For the arbitrary will of one it substitutes ordered rule and precedent. In place of the perplexities and fears and uncertainties that dog the steps of even the most brilliant autocrat, it enables men to forecast with safety the future and to earn their living in confidence and quietude. It provides the smooth and well-oiled machinery essential for those social inquiries and ameliorations which the modern conscience so insistently demands. In a word, it is the portal to modern democracy.

But woe to that country in which it is regarded, not as the gateway of government but as the goal itself! The hinges will grow rusty and the gate fast and immovable—a barrier to progress. In such a country, as in India, the sinister interests of the bureaucracy must ever more and more tend to usurp the rightful heritage of the people it governs. The criterion by which proposals will come to be approved or discarded will be, not so much the good of the governed as their effect on the prerogatives of the governors. Even when popular reforms are imposed by the supreme authority, they are apt to emerge from the bureaucratic workshop pale ghosts of the original design. As for the community itself, how can it possibly develop into a virile nation when persistently relegated to the position of little children divorced from all public affairs, divorced from all that makes for the soul of a people? Naturally in these circumstances manly virtues decay, docility and submission are all the vogue. It is not the freeman but the thrall whom the bureaucrat delights to honour. Every flash of independence will be snuffed out; only a nation of helots, brooding over past independence in a twilight of effete materialism, remains. Officials would no doubt deprecate such a consummation as the goal of their rule, but except in so far as that rule is modified and its aims amended by outside influences, it must undoubtedly produce that result. What avails it to prate of some vaguely remote self-government when all the time every act is sapping the virility that alone can make of self-government a success?

A practice once prevailed amongst certain Chinese of the baser sort, who were desirous of obtaining dwarfs for exhibition purposes, of placing kidnapped children in large earthen jars and of keeping them there for years until all growth had ceased. The unfortunates became dwarfs, not only in body but also in mind. Now, bureaucratic government, if long continued, acts like those jars. It so cramps and atrophies the life of a nation that, unless some happy accident comes to burst its trammels, no healthy growth can take place.

The superficial perfection of bureaucracy should not blind us to the more subtle permanent results, for it is by the results on a people's life that a government must be judged. If a majority of a people is effete, if they are wanting in courage or resource or self-respect, we will not call their government a good one. Still less ought we to accept the facile theory of official apologists, and ascribe to innate depravity results in reality due to a vicious polity. "Never let a prince," cried Machiavelli, "complain of the faults of a people under his rule, for they are due either to his own negligence or else to his own example." Bureaucrats in India may well ponder that saying in their hearts.

Fortunately for India, a movement has

arisen which promises to snap asunder the bonds of bureaucracy. Even to the heaviest sleeper the moment of awakening comes. This fact is apt to be forgotten by those who would have us believe that nations can be lulled into an eternal slumber. At first feebly, later with more vehemence, the tocsin of modern thought has sounded in the ears of India the Dreamer. She awakens from her long slumber and listens to new and wondrous thoughts, thoughts which can never fade away or die.

It was the Russo-Japanese war which finally electrified her into life. So long as all Asia bowed the knee to Europeans Indians could venerate them as superior beings, born into a higher plane than that in which they moved, without any great loss of self-respect. But when the Japanese, Asiatics like themselves, crushed in battle a great European power, and developed a civilization rivalling that of Europe, the scales dropped from their eyes. "If one nation armed with the panoply of Western knowledge can meet the West in equal rivalry, so also can we. If the Japanese can govern themselves creditably and with success on European lines, why, surely we, too, may achieve as much." Such are the not unnatural ideas which have permeated the educated class in India, and with such ideas the old-time acquiescence in the rule of strangers has for ever disappeared. In its place reigns the unrest that the short-sighted so deplore, an unrest quickened into rancour by official rebuffs, which dashes itself furiously against the impassive walls of the official hierarchy.

By an unfortunate coincidence, at the very moment when the Japanese victories thrilled into new life the advanced spirit in India that country was ruled by one who is the embodiment of all that is most inflexible in the bureaucratic mind. To screw down the safety-valve of an engine at the very time that steam is rising in the boiler can have but one result, and in India it was not long in coming. The bitterness and ill-will born of official repression have converted many critics of

British policy into foes to British rule. Their hostility is none the less perilous because veiled for the most part by Oriental secretiveness. The wide and varied tracts in which covert acts of sedition occur and the tone of the native press tell their own tale. Mistrust under an alien rule there must always be; discontent there must always be; but the depth and strength of the current of ill-will far surpass the limits which a statesman can view with equanimity or permit to exist without adequate remedy.

Added to the general unrest is the occurrence of sporadic outrages, the work of a gang of miscreants, whom it is the fashion to call anarchists. But they in no way hold by the tenets of anarchism properly so called; their aim is simply to embarrass the Government and to enforce their views by means of murder and outrage. No one styled the Moonlighters and Invincibles of Ireland anarchists. These Indian criminals derive their sole importance from two considerations. In the first place, they may provoke, and, in fact, have provoked, Government to reactionary measures and an attitude of stiff negation towards the proposals of the real reformers. In the second place, their very existence is diagnostic of grave disease in the body politic. Men such as they can no more multiply in an enlightened state than vermin on a clean skin. Anarchism properly so called has always failed to strike root in the free and happy soil of England; it flourishes only in countries, such as Spain and Italy, where the Government has utterly neglected the social condition of the people, or where it fails to give adequate expression to the popular will. So in India these sporadic outrages may well flash in our eyes a red danger-signal, a warning that Government has wandered gravely from the right path, that it is time to revise its course and to advance on altered lines.

Idle it is to denounce these criminals and to multiply large forces of secret police for their repression, unless we also, by broad and far-seeing measures, eradicate the conditions which have engendered them. In the absence of such remedies not only must these wretches pursue with occasional checks their criminal career, but, what is infinitely worse, a cloud of cold hostility to our rule will settle ever more closely over the land and harden men's hearts against us. Do not let us deceive ourselves by imagining that the old days of trusting acquiescence in our superior wisdom will ever return. They have gone for ever. It is childish to cry for the moon, and a very arid kind of moon at that. The only remedy, the only statesmanlike course, is to recognize frankly the strength of the new currents and to set the ship's course toward untried seas, which are so full of promise, so instinct with vivid life. The omens are propitious, if only we take heart of grace and follow them.

Will a bureaucracy, such as that which governs India, discern the menace of the times and set its house in order? Is it likely to meet and adjust itself to the altered conditions, and to govern on more popular and generous lines? The answer, one regrets to admit, must be an emphatic negative. If experience, if history teaches clearly any one lesson, it is that a bureaucracy will in no circumstances reform itself. If it is to be reformed at all, it must be by powers outside it and antagonistic to it. Apart altogether from the sinister interests which, in spite of pained protests, do sway officials, and do, perhaps unconsciously, influence their decisions, the force of mechanical routine is bound to prejudice them against any adequate system of reform. And if against reforms in general, how much more against reforms which must abrogate official prerogatives, undermine their authority, and transfer powers hitherto wielded by officials alone to the hands of the common people. A bureaucracy will never consent to such a profanation. It will oppose a hundred technical objections, a hundred difficulties and petty dangers which may conceivably wreck in practice any proposal for popular government. The average official forgets that, granted the principle is sound, time and experience can usually smooth away practical difficulties. Even when generous measures are imposed on a bureaucracy by the powers above, they are apt to suffer a sea change before being transmuted into the law of the land. We have seen this in the case of the Welby Commission; we have seen it in the rules under Lord Morley's Councils Act. Still less is it to be thought that officials, and in particular those trained in the secretariats, will, when appointed to high offices of control, conceive it their duty to inaugurate or to endorse a popular policy. Contrast the attitude of such to Lord Ripon on the one hand and to Lord Curzon on the other. In spite of plausible protests to the contrary, we must clearly recognize that a bureaucracy, as such, is, and from its nature will always be, hostile to a popular movement.

In India at the present day the gulf between officials and educated native opinion yawns ever wider, its depths fraught with sinister possibilities. To translate the position into terms of English politics, so long as India was Conservative, bureaucracy, apart from its subtle effect on their character, suited the people sufficiently well; now that the educated classes —the spear-head of the masses—have become Liberal, there is between them and their rulers a fatal clash of opinion. When a stiff and dry bureaucracy, manned by aliens, confronts nations whose educated classes and, to an increasing extent, whose masses are aflame with patriotic ardour, eager for measures of social betterment, and embittered by a thousand rebuffs and humiliations, it needs no prophet to forecast a catastrophe.

That is the present position in India. The question of questions is how best to bring into harmony these jarring elements of the body politic—in other words, how best to pave the way towards self-government, towards democracy. For democracy, though distant still as was Avalon to Sir Bedivere, is the goal towards which events irresistibly march.

Something may perhaps be done towards the formation of a Civil Service with more popular leanings. It can never become really democratic; the insistent influence of routine must inevitably crush the more generous impulses of the neophyte. But there is no need, as at present, to cradle competitors in an oligarchic nursery—for oligarchy is the half-sister of bureaucracy. The Universities of Oxford and Cambridge have justly earned a title to the respect and veneration of the English, alike through the breadth of their culture and through the illustrious and noble men who have drawn from them inspiration. But even their most devoted champions will hardly claim for them any democratic atmosphere. Though Socialists are not unknown in both universities, the universities have always stood for oligarchic as contrasted with democratic ideals; they have never put themselves at the head of any really popular movement. Popular movements are fain to find elsewhere their genesis and their inspiration. Now, the present rules for the Indian Civil Service, which were avowedly framed in the interests of these two Universities, inevitably tend to produce men imbued with such ideals, convinced supporters of exclusive rule. In view of the altered conditions, any such initial bias is much to be deprecated. In a perilous position, where success depends on a more democratic spirit, we are, in fact, weighting the scales against success ; where men with popular sympathies are becoming more and more needful, we take care to provide men imbued with the very contrary theories of government. If, too, as the falling off in competitors seems to indicate —in some recent years only three candidates competed for each vacancy—the raising of the age has struck out a large amount of quite legitimate material—the present rules have not even resulted in a higher intellectual standard. For more than one reason, then, a first step towards reform seems to lie in a lower age, with a lessened University training, for the Indian Civil Service.

In the framework of the Government itself, the Councils scheme devised by Lord Morley, however warped in execution, has achieved much. On the one hand it has created a forum in which educated natives may freely discuss their country's affairs; on the other, through a fresh breeze of informed criticism, it has cleared away many cobwebs from bureaucratic minds and enabled officials to see things more in their true perspective. Both Lord Minto and the Finance Minister, Sir J. Wilson, have frankly acknowledged that the new Councils are a powerful influence for good.

In cogency, in dignity of utterance, and in statesmanlike breadth of view the speeches of the unofficial members can bear comparison with those in the Imperial Parliament itself. They have singularly belied the forebodings of a host of officials and Anglo-Indians, who saw in the proposed reforms nothing but a weak concession to native "agitation" and a paltering with Imperial interests. Again and again in history has each concession of popular government been heralded by similar Cassandra-like wailings, which the event has utterly falsified. That does not, however, prevent their authors, forgetful of the past, from repeating their forebodings on each and every movement towards democracy.

The success of the Councils will hearten reformers to advance still farther in the same direction—in the direction, that is to say, of self-government by the people and for the people. This implies the relegation of the official hierarchy to its proper and subordinate place in the body politic. Like fire, bureaucracy may be a good servant, but it is a bad master. And the problem in the immediate future consists in the transfer of the supreme control to those who can see with other eyes than official ones, and whose ears are attuned to other music than official reports.

The reformation of the Councils was, as already stated, excellent. Its influence is abiding, and it is cumulative. The new Councils will go on from strength to strength, educating the people, and inspiring with a new spirit the strait and dusty secretariats of the Indian Governments. But the reform does not go far enough. To enforce the views and desires of the public, in opposition to the embattled host of officials, stand only five statesmen—namely, the Secretary of State, the Viceroy, and the Governors of Bombay, Madras, and Bengal—the latter quite a recent addition. These men have time and again proved their sterling worth; their influence has been priceless to steer the bark of government through deep waters. But they are not sufficient in themselves to withstand the constant official pressure. Either through direct opposition or by the poison of a more subtle suggestion, their well-meant reforms are too often whittled down into insignificant concessions. We have seen how the first Lord Elgin found his powers circumscribed and restricted. Even the transcendent personalities and the acumen of Lord Morley and James Mill have not availed to emancipate their minds from the web of suggestion so cleverly spun. Through this influence Lord Morley found himself betrayed into opposition of ideas and principles of which he has been the lifelong protagonist; through this influence Mill marred his work on Representative Government by a bizarre defence of Indian bureaucracy. There is no need now to enter into a discussion of his arguments, some of them based on erroneous premises, others rendered nugatory or obsolete by the lapse of time. The interest lies in the power of constant suggestion to pervert to official views so keen and shrewd a thinker as the younger Mill.

Clearly with these examples before our eyes it is necessary to strengthen the forces of the people, to reinforce the unequal battle. In the first place, the proportion of non-officials, preferably Indian, on the Council of the Secretary of State might well be increased to one-half. This will ensure due weight being given, in the discussion of great questions of policy, to the popular as opposed to the purely official views. And selected, as such men will be, for maturity of judgment and long experience, none need fear that "advanced" views will be unduly pressed upon the Secretary of State. It is not without reason that Huxley declared that all men over forty should be poleaxed.

A more radical change is called for in the Viceroy's Council, which is virtually his Cabinet. With the exception of the Commander-in-Chief, the Council should consist wholly of non-officials, chosen by the incoming Viceroy with the approval of the Secretary of State. Why should a Viceroy be compelled to work with a Cabinet the members of which may not be of his own choosing or to narrow his selection to a handful of officials? A Viceroy comes to India to carry out a particular policy; he holds certain views of government, and he sets before himself certain broad principles to which he desires to give effect during his tenure of office. Whether these views or principles be Conservative or Liberal it matters not. As has been already pointed out, there exists, and there will always exist, two divergent and irreconcilable theories of government. Each of these grand systems has its virtues; each has errors and excesses to which it is prone. But whatever be the Government in power in England, it is entitled, and its delegate the

Viceroy is entitled, to so select his Cabinet that he be unhampered in the execution of his policy, and derive from it that sympathetic assistance which men of like views can alone supply.

So much for the political aspect. But the administrative one is even more important. In England the great Secretaries or heads of departments are not chosen from the permanent officials, or from men who have had special training in the department concerned. Apart from political considerations, it is found that in practice broad matters of policy are best dealt with by Ministers who are unwarped by narrow departmental training, and who can discuss questions like men of the world with breadth and common sense. Why should not this be the case in India? Why should the ship be steered in India by the same hands as manipulate the intricate working of the machinery?

The selection of Ministers on the English model would also effect more than a dozen Decentralization Commissions to terminate the pettifogging interference which is the curse of the present administration of India. As long as the members of the Viceroy's Cabinet are officials they will act as officials, seeking to draw all the strings into their own hands, and lavishing on a million matters of detail that attention which should be devoted to great matters of state alone. Men of the world leave questions of detail to the disposal of the proper functionaries—that is, of the officials appointed to that end; we can imagine them quite incurious as to the price of a horse or the question of an extra bathroom. But to the really vital questions of policy, on which hang the destinies of a nation, to these they can bring a broad and generous outlook, such as one may look for in vain in the trained official. Nor do the benefits end here. With the relegation of the Government of India to the exercise of its proper functions, we shall probably also witness a drastic pruning of the India Secretariat. The economics under this head should constitute no mean boon in a country like India, where the expenditure on social betterment falls so miserably short of the needs of the people.

Although their terms of office should not be synchronous with that of the Viceroy, it seems advisable to appoint non-officials as the chiefs of provinces—with the exception, perhaps, of Assam—and thus still further to strengthen the non-official element in the administration. In fact, by the existence of the governorships of Bombay and Madras, and the recent creation of the governorship of Bengal, the principle has already been conceded; all that is required is its logical extension to the Punjab, the United Provinces, Bihar—that misshapen infant born out of due time—the Central Provinces, and Burma. Experience shows the practical advantage of such a reform; it introduces a broader, more popular, more sympathetic spirit into the provincial administration. True, even with such governors, the views of the official hierarchy will certainly predominate. But with the head of the province a non-official, we may legitimately expect greater flexibility, more attention to the interests of the people, especially to those interests that make for progress, and more harmonious relations between the British Government on the one hand, and the educated classes on the other. The reform, in short, is one which the times demand. It is a reform which a wise statesmanship will tender as a free boon, not as blackmail extorted by anarchy and violence.

For members of Council and governors of Provinces the Viceroy's choice may be expected to fall on men with parliamentary experience, or at least versed in English public affairs, and in the case of the former on leading Indian non-officials. The existing salaries and emoluments of these high offices seem sufficient to attract the right stamp of men. There is no reason why the change should add an anna to the burdens of India. Nor will it in any way derogate from the attractions of the Indian Civil Service. No single candidate joins that Service from any expectation of attaining one of these high offices, the prospects of appointment to which influence few outside a narrow clique of

Simla officials. If, as was recently alleged, the appointment of an " outsider " as member for Commerce caused discontent, we may be sure that the discontent existed only in the latter class, certainly not in the vast majority of the Service. For the most brilliant and devoted civilian numerous highly paid offices, apart altogether from those of members of Council or lieutenant-governors, offer an ample guerdon or reward. When these high appointments, in the interests of the nation it serves, shall have been withdrawn from amongst its prizes, that Service will stand, as it stands to-day, without parallel for rich emoluments and for the noble opportunities of distinction and high service it proffers to all who enter its portals.

Apart from the too limited power conferred on representatives of the public—a power which is, indeed, rather indirect than direct—the reformed Councils possess one rather serious defect. As was to be anticipated in any system in the forging of which the Government of India lent a hand, far too great weight and importance is given to the Viceroy's Council. The old serpent of bureaucratic centralisation, scotched in one place, uprears its head in another. If India is ever to develop on democratic lines, it is to provincial pride, to the love of one's province, that we must look. The vast extent of the sub-continent, the diversity of language and race and religion, chill and must always chill enthusiasm for a single Parliament. The Viceroy's Council men can regard at best with the cold respect vouchsafed to a House of Lords. It must always fail to touch their imagination and to quicken their patriotic ardour. For these purposes the system of provincial Councils holds the touchstone of success. Established on the broad foundation of common interests, it is from these Councils, and not that of the Viceroy, that the Indian Parliaments of the future will spring. Nor in the broad aspect could we wish it otherwise. For it is by diversity of development, not by mechanical uniformity, that federations of nations march forward and achieve greatness. Just as the variety of

States begemmed mediæval Italy with noble palaces, so may we look to local patriotism for the transfiguration of India. Let each of the great provinces have a free hand to work out its own salvation. Let them make their own experiments and learn by their own failures. Let the peoples of each province learn to take a pride in the development, both material and intellectual, of their province, engaging in a friendly rivalry with others as to which shall excel in the art of government. That way only salvation lies.

Now, as the English have long since discovered, you cannot have two co-equal legislative bodies; one or the other will tend to preponderate and to absorb the popular interest. Surely of the two councils, then, it is the provincial, and not the Viceroy's Council, which should hold pride of place. It is to them, and not to distant Simla or Delhi, that the people will look for the ventilation of grievances and the initiative in reforms.

Nothing is more likely to cramp the growing interest in the provincial Councils than the present practice, by which every act or resolution carried in them may be set aside by an inscrutable and distant bureaucracy. The remedy appears to be twofold. In the first place provincial Councils should receive much greater latitude to legislate in the provinces they represent. An unofficial majority may well constitute a normal feature of these Councils. The Viceroy's Council should, on the other hand, be reduced in number, and its legislative functions restricted to those subjects which concern directly or indirectly foreign Powers or in which a uniformity of procedure throughout India is really essential. (Such matters as police, arms, insurance—to take a few examples at random—certainly do not fall under this category.) That would be a measure of real and not merely formal decentralisation. Acts passed by the provincial Councils, except on certain defined subjects concerning which they might have plenary powers, should require the approval of the Viceroy's Council. They might be brought in by an official or non-official representing the province in question, according as the Act did or did not commend itself to the provincial governor. They could then, if desired, be fully discussed; and if rejected or amended by the official majority, the arguments for such rejection or amendment must needs be publicly and fully given. To borrow a judicial simile, the Viceroy's Council might have two functions: on the original side it might deal with certain matters concerning India as a whole; on the appellate side it might confirm, reject, or alter the acts of the provincial assemblies. In brief, it would constitute a second chamber of wide and exceptional powers, but still a second chamber. Such a Constitution, it may be argued, whilst retaining in the hands of the English Government all ultimate control and direction, would give free scope in the provincial Councils for political growth, and for that local patriotism which is the mainspring of all true political life.

Other minor reforms seem called for, such as the transfer of a portion of the power now wielded by district officers to the district Councils, whose position should be strengthened. The keynote to all progress lies, however, in the transfer of the superior control from the bureaucracy to men unwarped by official bias and more in sympathy with popular aspirations.

Once this major reform is achieved, the path of progress will lie open before us. It will be comparatively easy to advance with ordered steps toward the far-distant goal of democracy. And do not let us be deterred by the gloomy forebodings of those who see in every measure of justice to the people an unlocking of the floodgates of sedition. A thousand times has history belied such prophecies of disloyalty to the paramount Power. We may recall the saying of the Duke of Wellington on Canadian aspirations: "Their lordships may depend upon it that local responsible government and the sovereignty of Great Britain were completely incompatible." Or if that instance is too far off, the wailings of "men on the spot," like Lord Milner, before the grant of autonomy to South

Africa, should be fresh in our memories. The menace, the real peril, lies not in the grant of more popular government to India; it lies in the continuance of the present bureaucratic system, a system which has served its purpose but which India has now outgrown. That is the real danger, and it is one which those who prate of disloyalty will do well to consider very seriously. The great popular movement springing from the impact of Western knowledge and modern ideas, quickened into life by the war in the Far East, will neither ebb nor remain quiescent. On the contrary, it must wax from day to day, in spite of rebuffs and humiliations—nay, rather drawing fresh strength by each instance of official opposition. Of that we may be very sure, and, being sure, what is the only statesmanlike course to adopt? Is it to stand stolidly on the olden ways, to meet with cold denials the fervid aspirations of awakening India, to exhaust the armoury of repression in a futile effort to stem the advancing tide? Or should we not rather welcome with pride the increasing capacity of the Indians to govern themselves as the best proof of the justice and beneficence of our rule? Should we not rather recognize frankly that the time has come to release the Indians from leading-strings and to give scope, by suitable modifications in the constitution, to the development of a self-respecting people? Even those who harp most on expediency, that base expediency which has seldom more than of late perverted the minds of men, must recognize the wisdom of changing to meet changing conditions. Those—and we would fain believe they are the majority—who believe that the greatness of England lies, not in the subjugation of hordes of alien peoples, but in their elevation to greater moral heights, who see her glory, not so much in her Empire as in the free political ideals which inspire her in the administration of that Empire—all those will not hesitate in the course to adopt. Justice and expediency alike point out the road; it is for us now to march forward boldly, to hope and to dare.

And the members of the Indian Civil Service, easily the finest Service in the world, may recall with pride, even when handing over the sceptre of supreme control they have wielded so long, that their dominion in India has not been without its glories. To have replaced turbulence and disorder by peace, to have established courts of impartial justice, to have cast over the country a close network of roads and railways—all these are achievements which will ever redound to the honour of themselves and of England. But perhaps the greatest of boons, albeit an indirect one, which India has received at their hands has been the birth of a genuine spirit of patriotism. It is a patriotism which seeks its ideals, not in military glory or the apotheosis of a king but in the advancement of the people. Informed by this spirit, and strong in the material benefits flowing from British rule, India now knocks at the portal of democracy. Bureaucracy has served its purpose. Though the Indian Civil Service were manned by angels from heaven, the incurable defects of a bureaucratic government must pervert their best intentions and make them foes to political progress. It must now stand aside, and, in the interest of that country it has served so long and so truly, make over the dominion to other hands. Not in dishonour, but in honour, proudly, as shipbuilders who deliver to seamen the completed ship, may they now yield up the direction of India. For it is the inherent defects of the system, which no body of men, however devoted, can remove, which render inevitable the change to a new polity. By a frank recognition of those defects the Service can furnish a supreme instance alike of loyalty to the land of their adoption and of a true and self-denying statesmanship.